INTO THE UNKNOWN

INTO THE UNKNOWN

Harvey Day

BISHOPSGATE PRESS

© Harvey Day

ISBN 1-85219-030-2

British Library Cataloguing in Publication Data

Day, Harvey
    Into the unknown.
    1. Psychical research
    I. Title
    133   BF1031

    ISBN 1-85219-030-2 Pbk.

All enquiries and requests relevant to this title should be sent to the publisher, Bishopsgate Press Ltd., 37 Union Street, London, SE1 1SE

Printed by Whitstable Litho Ltd., Whitstable, Kent

CONTENTS

WHAT IS TIME?

Time has been defined as a fundamental directional aspect of experience, based on the direct experience of the duration of sensation, and on the experience of change from one sensory event, idea or train of thought to another. We distinguish this experience as having a beginning and an end; or a past, present and future. For practical purposes we impose limits on it in order that it can be measured. But time itself is illimitable.

We say that events that have taken place in the past cannot be reconstituted and that the future is unknown and cannot be seen.

This is not so, however, for the dead have been seen by those now living and events as yet to come about have been revealed in visions and dreams by those who possess second sight.* This has baffled, intrigued and frightened men since the dawn of civilization because there is no simple or satisfactory explanation for it.

Since the foundation of the Society for Psychical Research (SPR) in the middle of the nineteenth century investigators have probed this uncharted area, with comparatively little success, though within the past century many of our preconceived ideas have been shattered.

Measurement of Time

We like time to be measured accurately and scientists will go to incredible lengths to do so. Before the launching of the Soyuz-Apollo space craft in 1975, for instance, the pads were 16,000 km apart and it was imperative that the times at Cape Canaveral and Baikonur should coincide exactly. That was possible because both the Russians and the Americans had instruments that measured to infinitesimal fractions of a second. The Soviet standard of time and frequency for example, is measured by a complex device at the USSR Institute of Physico-Technical and Radio Engineering Measurements near Moscow, where the

*A supposed power by which occurrences in the future or things at a distance are perceived as if they were actually present.

7

standard clock strikes the second with an accuracy of one millionth of a microsecond and will take 30,000 years to build up an error of one second! It is impossible for the human mind even to conceive such an interval.

Units of time

All objects represent units of time. We can see some of them, such as flashes of lightning, taking place. A mountain represents a much larger unit of time for we cannot see either the beginning or the end, and there will come a day when the rocks and earth of which it is comprised will be washed into the sea and another mountain will rise from somewhere in the ocean bed.

Time is like a road which climbs to the top of a hill and disappears on the other side. The part behind us, that which has been lost to sight, represents the past; the stretch before us represents the present; that which falls from the brow of the hill and is hidden, is the future. Yet, like the road, every part of time – past, present and future – exists. Unlike the road, however, we cannot travel its entire length at will; that is, with the exception of a few highly sensitive people who are gifted, whom we call psychics* or clairvoyants**

Events are taking place all along our road and even though we cannot see them happening they are real. The past which we believe has vanished forever, has been retrieved by psychics and clairvoyants and the veil cast over the future has also been pierced by some.

Time Is Relative

Time is relative, for though the actual units may be the same, a period may itself appear long or short, depending on the circumstances and the individual concerned. Time may appear to fly during an examination in which one has a great deal to say and a limited time in which to satisfy the examiners; time flies while watching an exciting game, an enthralling film or play, or in congenial company, especially that of a person with whom one is in love. It drags interminably while waiting in a dentist's

*Psychic: from the Greek word for soul or life; one who is susceptible to spiritual influence.

**Clairvoyant: derived from the Latin clarus, clear; and videre, see; the gift possessed by psychics of seeing the forms and hearing the voice of those who have passed over.

surgery, at the end of a long queue in a supermarket, or while stranded on a ledge on a cliff waiting to be rescued, with the tide coming in. In some instances a few minutes seem to drag into hours – even an eternity – and such periods cannot be measured in chronological time.

We are told that dreams during which a whole series of events take place, occupy only a few seconds. The idea, however, that when drowning the entire past unravels before one's eyes like a film, is false. When I was a boy in my teens my friends and I sometimes went swimming in a lake which had an island in the middle. At the time I could not swim so I sat in the middle of a long plank while the others towed it to the island. On the return trip they all suddenly dived away when we were in deep water and I was left to paddle. Then one end of the plank started to go under and I soon found myself in the water, struggling to keep afloat. I went under again and again and could see the sun shining brilliantly, as if it were on the horizon. The next thing I knew was that I was ashore; they turned me upside down and the water was coming out of me with a rush. But not a single event of the past had appeared to me. What concerned me most was that my mother should never hear of my misadventure or it would have been the worse for me.

Time has baffled man throughout the centuries. St. Augustine was perplexed my it. 'What is time,' he cried; 'if nobody asks me, I know; yet if I am asked, I do not know.'

Time means different things to different people. In his *Letters to My Son* Chesterfield urges: 'Know the true value of time; snatch, seize, and enjoy every moment of it. No idleness, no laziness, no procrastination; never put off till tomorrow what you can do today.'

I am more in true, however, with W. H. Davies, the Tramp Poet, who wrote:
'What is life if, full of care
We have not time to stand and stare?'

Dr. Soal's Experiments

Psychics do not know why they can see into the future, or into the past; they merely have some in-built apparatus which enables them to do so. Investigators such as Dr. J. B. Rhine of Duke University, South Carolina, and Dr. S. G. Soal of Queen Mary College, London University, have conducted thousands of experiments to find out whether normal people with no claim to being psychic, can also see into the future. In 1941 he and Whately Carrington re-examined the records of 160 people who had made guesses with zener cards* and found that two of these subjects made guesses far beyond the possibilities of co-incidence. One of them, Shackleton, guessed correctly at least two seconds *before* the next card was lifted from the top of the pack. He made 250 guesses in all, each time naming the next card two seconds before it was handled. This was no proof that he could see into the future but it was an indication that he possessed some abnormal instinctive sense.

But, if two seconds ahead, why not ten or a hundred?

Chronological Time

In the dim past the sun was the only clock. When I was a boy in Eastern Bengal labourers worked from sunrise to sundown, breaking off at mid-day when the sun was at its zenith. In Ancient Egypt they placed a staff in the ground and as the sun made its journey from east to west, measured time by its shadow. Those were the first sun dials. Later in Europe, hour glasses filled with sand were used to determine limited periods of time. Then the first clocks were made and installed in church towers to regulate the life of the community, and on the sabbath men were summoned to church by the tolling of bells. Finally the watch was devised and time was divided into hours, minutes and seconds, making man the slave of time. Today our lives are chained to the clock.

Even so, chronological time is sometimes defeated by the age of a person. The young who live fast, find that time hangs and physiological time means different things to the young and the old. Wounds suffered by boys of ten heal four times as fast as those of a man of 50, for boys' cells multiply far more rapidly and broken and dead tissues are renewed much faster. But strangely enough, whereas in youth time hangs and the years drag, after 50 they appear to fly.

In a year the change in a boy in his teens may seem remarkable. He may have grown inches, and broadened and filled out; but between 50 and 55 there may be no noticeable change in a man. So though the youth's metabolism may be

Zener cards: named after their inventor. Five cards bearing simple diagrams. A pack consists of 50 with 10 of each kind.

10

much faster time passes much more slowly than with a man. A curious paradox.

Defeating Time

Sometimes psychics seem to be able to traverse time backwards and forwards. That they possess some power which normal people do not have has been proved by instruments that measure the electrical radiations emitted by their bodies; but there is as yet no means of measuring how much greater are the radiations produced by one psychic than another; nor do we know the source of such radiations. Some psychics can turn this power off and on at will.

Psychic Power and Inspiration

In some respects psychic power resembles what we call inspiration. Psychologists term this state *subliminal precognition*, which though originally used by psychoanalysts to denote an unconscious process by which a sexual impulse, or its energy, is deflected, so as to express itself in some non-sexual and socially acceptable activity, today it is often used loosely for any substitution of what appears to be a higher satisfaction for a lower. It is a state below the threshold of perception; employed either of stimuli, or stimulus differences. Sometimes it can be generated or developed by a habit, such as study, or the acquisition and marshalling of knowledge where the subject is confronted by a mass of facts, apparently unrelated, which in themselves mean little, but suddenly, like the pieces of a jig-saw, fall into place revealing the entire picture.

Also in some respects but not in others, inspiration resembles precognition. Neither can be forced. Inspiration, which is usually the result of hard work and acquired knowledge, bursts on one when the mind is completely at rest and not engaged on work; precognition is also a sudden and unexpected phenomenon. Both are undoubtedly governed by natural laws which as yet we do not understand. The ability to recall the past like the re-showing of a film, or to see into the future, is not one that normal mortals can command at will. Kenneth Odhar, seer to the Lords of Seaforth and Clan Mackenzie, known as the Brahan Seer, used a "gazing stone" through which he looked, in order to raise the levels of the subconscious and see what was hidden from other people.

SEEING INTO THE PAST

A peep into the future is what most people want when they visit palmists, astrologers and clairvoyants. The first two do not rely on psychic gifts but on data derived from scrutinising the palm in the first instance; and the date, time and place of birth in the second. The clairvoyant alone is dependent on psychic gifts.

But no one pays to see into the past, which is already known, unless he happens to be a detective who is trying to discover the whereabouts of a missing person whom he has cause to believe has been murdered, and in rare instances clairvoyants have been able to help.

Sometimes, however, events from the past have been revealed to those now living, whether they want to see them or not. They have no control whatever, of the mechanism or processes which produce the past. These events flash into the subconscious either in the form of dreams, or into the conscious mind in the form of visions. The most common of such revelations is the ghost or apparition which, though rarely doing any harm, is usually feared because it confronts one so unexpectedly and more often than not when alone and at night, for men have an atavistic fear of the dark, which is associated with demons and other fearsome beings. Fear of the unknown is common to most humans.

Turning Back The Pages of History

For no reason that one can advance there are people who have been confronted by vivid scenarios from the past. One of the best known instances is that recorded in a little book called *An Adventure* published in 1911. The authors were two distinguished scholars, C. Anne E. Moberly, Principal of St. Hugh's College, Oxford, and Eleanor F. Jourdain, a member of her staff who eventually succeeded her.

While travelling in France in August 1901 during the Long Vacation, they visited the Petit Trianon at Versailles. They were puzzled for the place did not fit in with their expectations. The buildings were not where their maps placed them and some of the buildings were not on the maps at all! The air was so still and oppressive, even for that month, that both women, neither of whom was a neurotic type, felt like screaming with nervousness akin to terror. They couldn't account for it.

The gardeners and others whom they saw bore little resemblance to living people for they wore the garments of a generation long past and spoke archaic French. They watched a pretty woman dressed in a long outmoded cape, sketching in one of the gardens, and a vicious looking fellow with a pock-marked face followed them everywhere. He scared them. There was also something so eerie about the place that they left as soon as they could and were greatly relieved when they got outside.

Later they returned to the Petit Trianon and to their astonishment found it to be utterly transformed.

They mingled with crowds of gay tourists all dressed in fashions then in vogue, and the gardeners and gendarmes seemed normal and pleasant. The Petit Trianon they had seen on their previous visit had vanished. They couldn't understand it.

With scholarly care they compared the old maps and fashion books with the scenes of their first visit and to their astonishment found that the situations of the buildings and the dresses, coincided with those of their vision. They then carried out an exhaustive correspondence with French historians and other authorities and as a result were convinced that they had seen the Petit Trianon exactly as it had been in the reign of Marie Antoinette round about the year 1789! The documents they provided to substantiate their theory, now housed in the Bodleian Library, were taken seriously by scholars in Oxford and in Paris.

Why were they shown this facet of history, for neither woman had any claim to being psychic?

Plurality of Times

We assume that there is only one dimension of time but Emmanuel Kant suggested that our conception may be due to a special pattern in which our sensory apparatus has evolved and the true order of the universe might be something quite different.

There have been innumerable theories to explain this and

many books have been written about them: *Looking Backwards* by Edward Bellamy; *The Time Machine* by H. G. Wells; *Nothing Dies* by J. W. Dunne; in which he developed the theory of serialism. Dunne suggested that reality as it appears to science, has to be a series of regresses which stretch back into infinity so that nothing that ever happened is lost. In *Time and The Conways,* J. B. Priestly elaborates this theory.

Dunne suggested that the time barrier does not exist and is merely a creation of consciousness, but that the subconscious pay no attention to the time barrier. That is why the past comes back so vividly and accurately in dreams, and why ghosts which the sensitive can see, are realities from the past.

If this is admitted the "time-moment" which we believe exists for a mere fraction of a second and then dies forever, is something that will have an existence for all eternity. If fact, everything exists forever.

There are scores of well authenticated cases where the past has been seen with vivid distinctness and entire slabs of history have been revealed a century or more after the events had taken place. Why and how are still questions which remain un-answered and which will be for many a year.

The Man Who Saw Yesterday

Most of us are concerned with what will happen in the future; whether economic crises will be solved, elections won, or wars brought to satisfactory conclusions. Few except historians, teachers and writers are concerned with the past. Even the events of today are quickly relegated to the past. But sometimes events from the past are flashed on to the screen of the mind with such reality that the eye can see them. And if the eye can see them there is some justification for assuming that the past has not been entirely obliterated.

Men and women have dreamt of crimes already committed; dreams that showed in detail the locality of the crimes, the faces and forms of the victims, and those who killed them.

These details are conveyed to the dreamers' minds as if actually taking place and with such accuracy that the police have been led to the places where murders have been committed.

What apparatus it is that can transpose a picture from the past and transplant it in a dreamer's mind, we do not know. If the past no longer exists, this should be impossible for according to the school of Satre the mere existence of something is proof that it must be.

One of the most extraordinary cases of regression occurred on a hot summer's day between the years 1746–1753, the nearest that Archibald Bell, a farmer of Inveraray, could place the event, which he recorded many years later. Bell wrote it down exactly as told to him by his father and grandfather, whose farm he inherited.

'On the morning of the day mentioned, my Grandfather having occasion to transact some business in Glenshiray, took my Father along with him. They went there by crossing the Hill which separates it from Glenshiray, and their business in Glenshiray being finished a little later after mid-day, they came round by Garron Bridge in order to return home. At the time the road generally used from Glenshiray to Inveraray lay on the west side of the river Shiray, all the way to the Garron Bridge, where it joined the high road, being then (as you know) within view of a part of the old town of Inveraray, which has since been demolished and the Ground upon which the new Town stands, and of the whole line of road leading from it, to the above mentioned bridge, they were very much surprised to behold a great number of Men under Arms marching on foot towards them.'

The front ranks had advanced only as far as Kilmalieu in regular order, packed close, and according to the writer 'they stretched from the point of the New Town near the Quay where Captain Gillies' house now stands, along the shore and the high road and across the River Aray near the Town, about the spot where the new bridge has since been built.'

The Army stretched so far into the distance that the rearguard could not be seen.

As it advanced slowly towards them the old man noted that it had 15 or 16 pairs of colours and that the men marching nearest to them were walking six or seven abreast. With them marched, as was the custom, women and children, both above and below the road, carrying cans and other cooking utensils.

The men were clad in scarlet, the glinting sun on their muskets and bayonets dazzling the Bells; and somewhere in the middle distance was a large animal amid the ranks, being urged on by prods from knives and bayonets.

Young Bell had never seen as large a body as an army before as

15

armies rarely ventured into the remote Highlands, but his father who had served during the Rebellion of 1745, assumed that they had come from Cantyre and were making their way south to England.

One peculiarity struck his son. 'Why,' he asked; 'are the rear ranks constantly running to catch up with those in front?'

His father explained that there was always confusion in the middle of an army, which in those times proceeded like mobs; so the rear ranks were constantly being delayed and as a result forced to hurry to keep their positions. 'If ever you get into the army;' he advised; 'always try to join the front ranks, which march at a leisurely pace and are never held up.'

The army was now about 150 yards from them and they could see distinctly a body of some 40–50 men led by an officer on foot a little way behind.

A few paces behind him rode an officer of Dragoons – or so they concluded from the trapping of his horse. He wore a gold laced hat and a blue Hussar cloak with wide open sleeves lined with red material; boots and spurs. Bell senior observed him so intently as to swear later that he would know him again instantly if ever they met.

At that period all able-bodied men went in fear of press gangs who forced them not only into the Navy but into the Army as well, so young Bell felt it inadvisable to linger on the road for he had no wish to spend many years in foreign lands. Both scaled a stone dyke behind some thorn bushes, and thus safely screened watched the army march by. Then suddenly, the road which a few moments ago had been thronged by men, was deserted!

Young Bell rubbed his eyes and asked his father to look but never a sign of men in uniform could they see. Then it occurred to the old man that there had been no cloud of dust, which on broken roads was always created by men, beasts and vehicles. So they clambered over the dyke and on to the road where they saw an old resident of Glenshiray named Stewart, coming towards them, driving a horse. 'What has become of all the soldiers?' they asked.

'What soldiers?' said Stewart; 'I've seen none.' All the information he volunteered was that as the heat had made his horse sag from fatigue, he had dismounted and was driving it. It was the same animal they had seen in the midst of the throng!

To his dying day Farmer Bell believed that their vision had been a peep into the future but his son said that the uniforms and the arms carried by the men belonged to the past. It may be added that both were abstemious and had taken no refreshment stronger than milk before setting out for home. They examined the road for footprints but could see none; they made guarded inquiries from local folk about a visiting army, but no one had seen a single soldier. So Archibald Bell made careful and accurate notes of everything they had seen that afternoon and sent them to Colonel Campbell, whom he knew, and Campbell passed them on to the Duke of Argyll who had them published in the *Pall Mall Magazine.*

Edith Olivier's Vision

Edith Olivier, the writer, was extremely sensitive and psychic. One projection into the past by her has been recorded by David Herbert, second son of the Earl of Pembroke, in his book *Second Son,* and also by Brigadier C. A. L. Brownlow, DSO, whose wife was psychic as well.

While Edith Olivier was driving home from a Council meeting one evening the mist came down so thickly that she was about to turn back when she saw an avenue of monoliths. As she was a historian who had written about Wiltshire she realized she must have been near Avebury, which had been built among the remains of a Druid temple. So she followed the line of the avenue, thinking it would lead her to Avebury.

Then she heard music, so stopped and got out of the car. Everything seemed plain. There was no mist and, to her astonishment a fair was in progress and the villagers, in fancy dress, were singing and dancing to tunes which seemed strangely old fashioned. After watching for some minutes she thought nothing of it and drove home, but recorded the incident in detail in her diary.

Twenty years later, however, she attended a meeting of the Archaeological Society in Salisbury where the Committee were deciding where to search for a lost avenue of monoliths leading to Avebury. 'Oh,' interrupted Edith Olivier; 'I can take you there now!' She went on to describe what she had seen twenty years earlier.

Naturally, they were sceptical, so she asked them to wait while she drove three miles to her home and returned with her diary. When she read the extracts they were impressed. They were even more convinced when the Chairman read out a passage from an old book which stated that every year until 1840 a fair had been held on the identical spot and on the same night of the year on which Edith Olivier had seen her vision. Subsequent excavation unearthed the monoliths which made up the avenue. They had sunk with the years and were several feet below the surface.

Mrs. Brownlow's Peep Into The Past

Brigadier Brownlow's wife also had frequent peeps into the past. 'On one occasion,' he relates; 'two years ago, when in Paris staying at an hotel near the Palais Royal, a similar event occurred, but in this instance I myself heard, though I did not observe, a scene from the past.

'I suddenly was awakened by a loud smashing or rending noise, like the breaking of wood. I jumped out of bed half asleep, shouting: "There's a man in the room!" My wife was also awakened.

'However, all was quiet both in the street outside and in the house. I switched off the light, and before going to sleep we discussed the noise, which my wife described as a tremendous smashing noise which seemed to come from a large heavy wardrobe.

'Then my wife began to see clairvoyantly. She said she saw the whole of the room but with decorations and furniture of a different order.

'In the centre of the room was a young girl with powdered hair, dressed in a rich costume of a past age. Her hands were holding a large harp.

'Then my wife heard soft and lovely music, not from the harp but of violins. She was fascinated by this scene, looking and listening with interest; but except for the initial smashing noise, I heard nothing.

'I instituted inquiries next day and was informed that the part of the house we occupied had been unaltered for centuries; and in the time of Louis XIV had been in possession of a prominent courtier of that period.'

That does not, of course, constitute proof of anything; but for both of them to have heard the smashing noise and for Mrs. Brownlow to have seen a vision from the past and heard the music of violins leads one to believe that a tiny facet of a bygone age had been revealed. Brigadier Brownlow must also have been somewhat psychic otherwise he would not have heard the noise; so it is apparent that some people are more psychic than others.

Because we do not understand how others can see and hear events which took place years ago we call them freaks. Dr. Henry Sigerist, of Johns Hopkins Medical School, one of the leading authorities in his day, said: 'It is very unscientific to deny the experience of 2,000 years merely because we have no ready made theory that explains all phenomena in detail. It would have been foolish to deny the existence of lightning because electricity was not yet known. Experience has preceded science more than once.'

Professor Littlejohn

Professor J. J. Littlejohn, formerly of Oxford University, was a freak. He had a brain like a radio receiving station, for he could see colour, and receive thoughts and brain waves through the air. 'As a boy,' he said; 'I used to sit on the cliffs of Devon and gaze at the ships that sailed there *centuries* ago. I could sense animal life underground and see it telepathically.'

Frequently he disconcerted visitors by telling them exactly what they did before coming to see him. 'You left home,' he would say; 'by the back gate, walked through a muddy lane, caught a bus, stood all the way in a crowded train next to a woman in a red hat and had a cup of coffee and two biscuits in a tea shop before coming here.'

Invariably he was right.

He sometimes helped friends to trace articles they had mislaid or lost. He told a woman whose jewels had been stolen, exactly what had happened to them, and added they would be replaced by the person who had taken them. They were.

He also traced a missing man telepathically and said he was in Australia. He was found there.

He could see into the past and across oceans and continents. Once when a friend lost a ring he led him into a wood through which he had walked; then stood and pointed. There it lay.

The Coming Of The Vikings

More than 1,000 years ago the Vikings sailed across the North

Sea, landed on our shores at various points from the Hebrides to East Anglia, slaughtered the inhabitants, sacked their homes and looted their possessions. There are many in the Highlands and in the Hebrides today who are fey and claim to have seen the Norsemen. Johnnie MacMillan, for instance, a prominent member of the Iona community, set out one fine evening to call on Mrs. Fergusson, an old lady renowned for her gift of second sight and her prophetic powers, who lived in a croft about half a mile away. He had traversed the straight round road many a time but on that evening discovered to his amazement that there was no sign of the croft, in fact, the road deemed different. So he continued along it to White Sands. Here he came to a halt for there was not a sign of the croft belonging to his friend. It was Mid-Summer Day and still daylight, for the sun scarcely sets in those northern latitudes.

When he reached the bay he stopped to let the peace and tranquillity of the evening seep into his soul. Then suddenly he stopped spellbound, for from behind Eilaen Annraidh, a rock-bound island off the coast, he saw a fleet of war galleys propelled by brawny Norsemen cutting through the water and making for the shore.

He counted 14 long narrow boats with high prows and sterns and could see the warriors in the galleys shouting to each other, though he could not hear them. It was as if he was watching a silent film.

The invaders leapt ashore and dragged their boats up on to the beach. About 50 yards from where he stood was a group of ashen-faced Columbian monks, at whom the raiders rushed. They were massacred to a man. The Vikings then disappeared towards the Abbey and soon after reappeared driving before them a herd of cattle belonging to the order. Then with their booty aboard, they leapt into their vessels and rowed out to sea.

As he looked on MacMillan could see the glow of the flames from the burning Abbey, for the Vikings invariably burnt what they could not take.

As the invaders rowed off he could see distinctly the big square sails decorated with emblems; their colours and designs.

It was then about eleven o'clock and though the light was receding he was still able to see fairly well, so he drew an old envelope from a pocket and made rough sketches of the designs on the back. Then the scene obliterated and old familiar landmarks were suddenly renewed.

MacMillan sent a full account of his vision, together with his sketches, to the British Museum, and a few weeks later the authorities replied saying that incidents such as he had seen probably took place round about the twelfth century. A contemporary account written in Latin confirms, in fact, an invasion on White Sands on Christmas Eve 986, when 15 monks were slaughtered, their cattle driven into the galleys and the Abbey gutted and ruined.

Another who saw a similar incident was F. C. B. Cadell, a well known Edinburgh artist. While painting near the Hermit's Cave, a grotto not far from the north end of the island, he suddenly realized that a battle was going on around him. Though he could see the combatants hacking at each there was no sound of battle. So disturbed was he that though a man of strong will and sound nerves, he decided to leave the spot at once.

Other inhabitants of Iona have witnessed what is known as "The Sight:" the phantom ships, the landing of the Vikings, and the massacre of the monks and the violation of the Abbey.

Thomas A. Edison, most prolific of all modern inventors, believed that energy, like matter, is indestructible and that vibrations never die. It was one of his many ambitions to build a machine that would be able to recapture past conversations, music and other sounds from the ether and replay them for the edification and amusement – and possibly the education – of lay audiences and scientists. But he died before he could get round to it.

Sir Cecil E. Denny

Another who believed in the theory that nothing ever dies was Sir Cecil E. Denny, head of the North-West Mounted Police (the Mounties) of Canada. His theory was reinforced by an unusual experience, which he described in his book *Riders of The Plain*, published in 1885.

In 1875 when he was a young police officer stationed at Fort Walsh in Rupert's Land which in 1905, was divided into the provinces of Alberta and Saskatchewan, he set out accompanied by an Indian guide on a hunting and fishing trip 40 miles up the Oldman River. They took a packhorse, blankets, cooking utensils and a collapsible rubber dinghy, for when they reached their destination Denny intended to send his guide back by the overland route and make his way home downstream, for he loved the water and was an expert in handling boats.

On his return journey, however, he was overtaken by a violent storm with winds of hurricane force, lightning and terrifying peals of thunder. Though it was four in the afternoon on a mid-summer's day the sun was blotted out and it was almost pitch dark; so he paddled for the shore, hauled his boat up the bank and sheltered in a thick clump of timber. After a while the storm abated and to his astonishment and delight he could hear the rhythmical thump-thump of Indian drums and the monotonous chanting of their familiar 'hi-ya, hi-ya, hi-ya, hi-ya.'

As he was soaked to the skin he decided to make for the encampment where he was sure of food, a hot drink and a fire to dry his clothes. As he approached the sound he could see the teepees with their gaudy decorations and realized that they were Crees, who were good friends of the police.

Then he saw a number of copper skinned men, some dressed in cast off white men's clothing, others in nothing but a breech clout, moving about unperturbed by the rain, thunder or lightning. The squaws were preparing meals and attending to their little brown papooses who frolicked naked, as children do the world over; and behind the camp horses grazed contentedly, unworried by the furious tempest.

This seemed strange and out of character for he knew that during storms the Indians invariably closed their tent flaps, for they feared thunder which they imagined to be the fury of the gods. As by this time the camp was only about 100 yards away he decided to sprint towards it but the instant he got beyond the fringe of timber he found himself enveloped in a sheet of flickering, bluish, electrical flame and was hurled to the ground where he lay for a time, senseless.

On regaining consciousness he was unable to rise and lay helpless for an indefinite period as the rain beat down on him. Eventually he struggled to his feet and staggered towards the camp – but to his astonishment there was no camp in sight; not a tent or a man or a woman. The children he had seen gambolling had vanished; so had the horses; and an eerie silence replaced the thumping of the drums and the chorus of 'hi-ya, hi-ya!' He examined the ground on which the wigwams had been pitched and the paddock where the horses had grazed but there was never a sign of a footmark, a hoof-print, or a blade of grass trodden underfoot. The area looked as if it had been undisturbed for many years.

As he was about to return to the shelter of the wood a shaft of lightning struck a massive tree, splitting it from top to bottom, so rather than risk being struck he decided to return to Fort Walsh on foot and not by boat as intended.

It was past midnight when he covered the 15 miles and arrived utterly exhausted. He then bathed, hung up his wet clothes to dry and slipped between warm blankets.

Next morning when he related his experiences to brother officers his leg was pulled unmercifully; but later that day, accompanied by an Indian guide, he returned to the scene of his vision, to retrieve his boat, and this time the scene was completely transformed. The country was bathed in warm sun and in the distance he could see the foothills of the Rockies. The sole evidence of his strange adventure was the tree that had been struck by lightning.

He went over the camp site, examining it carefully and could discern rings of stones overgrown by grass where a camp had been pitched many years ago. Bleached bones were scattered about and he found two skulls; one an adult's and the other that of a child. The Indian guide then explained that in his father's day a band of Crees had camped there and were attacked by an overwhelming force of Blackfeet who were their natural enemies. Taken by surprise, every man, woman and child had been slaughtered. Their wigwams were burnt and their horses stolen.

Denny, who was a reliable officer not given to flights of imagination, eventually inherited the Irish baronetcy of Tralee, but remained in Canada, attained a high position in the force and retired in 1886, after which he was offered a post with the Department of Indian Affairs, and later was appointed Archivist to the Government of Alberta. He died in 1928 at the age of 78, but not before he had written a detailed account of his strange adventure.

Spectator To A Battle

Another who was privileged to witness a scene from the past was Paul Smiles who in 1959 lived in Nairobi, Kenya. One fine morning, accompanied by an African tracker, he set forth to shoot a pride of lions that had raided native stock corrals and thus had placed themselves outside the bounds of protective game laws.

When they reached the locality where the lions were supposed to be lurking they finished supper and as darkness was about to descend they climbed high into *machans* (platforms) set up in the branches of two tall trees about 100 yards apart, which their guide had constructed months earlier. 'Be careful,' he warned as Smiles was about to ascend his ladder; 'the ropes (made of vines and saplings) may have rotted.' Then the tracker made for his tree, and the pair settled as comfortably as they could, using the tree trunks as back rests.

It was close to full moon and in its strong light they could see clearly the pools where animals came down to drink. The light in fact was so strong that its reflected glare off the surface of the pool dazzled Smiles and made it difficult for him to concentrate on the spot.

Towards midnight it grew chilly so he drew his blanket round him and soon could no longer keep his eyelids from drooping. But he had not been dozing long when a roar drove sleep from his eyes and etched in the bright moonlight were a group of lions which looked much nearer than they really were. They walked to and fro as if sensing danger, their tails lashing ominously. They approached the pool in small rapid dashes in twos and threes, then stopped, shoulder to shoulder. As they were no more than 50 yards from the pool they would soon be within easy range. Smiles eased off his blanket, made himself comfortable, took up a firing position and steadied his rifle. The African had agreed that Smiles should take the first shot.

The leader of the pack, a massive creature with a huge dark mane, strode out in front and stopped within a few yards of the water. Smiles took careful aim and just as he was about to press the trigger the crack of a rifle shot came from the direction of the tree in which the tracker was installed. The alarmed beasts scattered in panic, soon to be lost in the bush.

At that moment the thunder of battle broke the silence and volley after volley of rifle fire crashed around him. It seemed as if hundreds of men were involved. In between the volleys he heard commands both in English and German! These were followed by further fusilades and shouted commands – then silence.

On looking down he saw Simbia Mia Mbili, his guide, at the foot of the tree. 'Did you shoot?' he asked, knowing before the words were out of his mouth that the question was unnecessary.

'No, Bwana,' replied Simbia.

'Then who . . .?'

In a mixture of pidgin English and Swahili he explained; 'I did not expect you to shoot a lion, Bwana; not on this night, which is the night of the War Fight that took place here 25 years ago between your soldiers and their enemy, the Germans. I have gone through it twice before and I couldn't believe what I heard. I thought it was some kind of nightmare. I dare not tell anyone about it. They would have thought I had been bewitched by an enemy I was unaware of. At last I could stand it no longer and that is why I got the courage to bring you, a soldier, here tonight to see if you could hear what I heard. Now that you have heard it in the same way as I did, I feel better Bwana, I do.' Then beckoning Smiles to follow, Simbia said: 'Come with me. I want to show you something.'

With that he led him to a rise in the open veldt where stood rows of weather beaten crosses that marked the graves of British and Germans who had fallen in that encounter. Outnumbered by more than ten to one the British had been annihilated but had obviously given a good account of themselves as the toll of Germans was extremely heavy. 'Since then,' Simbia explained; 'the ancient enemies return to fight their battle again.'

There have been recorded many similar incidents, of battles being re-fought, the best known being the phantom Battle of Edgehill, during the English Civil War, which has been witnessed not once, but time and again; by crowds of peasants, clergy, gentry, and at least three of the King's Officers in Northamptonshire.

Why these visions are seen, why they sometimes recur, and why some can see them and others not, are questions unlikely to be answered for many a day. But that they take place is on record. Nor are all who see them psychic. Smiles, for instance, laid no claim to extra-sensory powers; nor could the peasants who witnessed the spectral battle of Edgehill. Some other reason must be advanced.

In the January number of the *Cosmopolitan Magazine* in 1960 Eugene D. Fleming put forward the theory that such phantoms have nothing to do with survival after death but recur because of a "psychic ether" which is something like "an ethereal TV tape" on which everything is recorded and which, when conditions are favourable, records and plays back incidents which took place in the past. Which can neither be proved nor disproved, except that some sort of apparatus is needed to play back the tape. And this was not available in places where visions have been seen.

Many theories have been advanced to explain regression, for it isn't only the crackpots who believe that the past can be brought back and revealed as clearly as a picture on a colour television screen.

Sir Oliver Lodge's Theory

Sir Oliver Lodge was Principal of Birmingham University, a President of the British Association, a Fellow of The Royal Society, and distinguished for his examination of the ether and his work on radio telegraphy. He was also famous (or notorious) for his interest, and belief in, the occult. When Dr. Frederick Barnardo, a distinguished physician and at one time Dean of the Medical Faculty of the University of Calcutta, related to him an experience of regression, Lodge said that in his opinion the molecular arrangement of the atmosphere is disturbed by events and if at some later date the exact patterns can be reproduced at the same spot and under the same climatic conditions, the events will be exactly duplicated though the chances of this taking place may be many billions to one. But there have been occasions when such conditions were reproduced and Dr. Barnardo describes such an experience.*

A Slice of History Enacted

In 1903 when Barnardo was Medical Officer attached to the 11th Lancers in India, he was ordered to make his way to Delhi to attend Lord Curzon's Durbar. It was evening and though dusk gathered, the full moon was rising and in the tropics moonlight is often brilliant enough to enable one to read the small print of a newspaper.

Suddenly, approaching a slight rise in the road, he saw four elephants walking abreast. For a moment he could hardly believe the evidence of his eyes. Four ponies trotted behind the elephants. Though they were still some hundreds of yards away

*An Active Life: Dr Frederick Barnardo

his horse grew restive so he dismounted and sheltered behind a clump of mahogany trees from where he could see what turned out to be a procession.

When the head of the procession came into line with him he could see the tail stretching back in the full moonlight, for half a mile. On each of the elephants was perched a drummer who kept up a monotonous beat while the throng behind him chanted a mournful 'Hi! Hi! Hi!'

The riders on the ponies were four young nobles. This he could see from their *pugarees* (turbans) which were blue, yellow, red and pink respectively, and by the clothes they wore.

Suddenly the drumming and the chanting ceased and the silence became so oppressive that he feared that his breathing and that of his horse could be heard by them.

Behind the horsemen were four *doolies* or *palkees* (palanquins) with their jhilmils (shutters) open. He could see that the occupants, who looked mournful, were high caste ladies.

On the verge of the road a group of wrestlers and acrobats were limbering up and performing handsprings and somersaults. Fire-eaters and dancers gyrated and went through their customary evolutions; but not a sound came from any of them. It seemed like a silent colour film.

Then as suddenly, the silence was shattered. An English officer galloped to the head of the procession while his aide hung back. During his stay in India Barnardo has seen many uniforms but none like the ones worn by the Englishmen, which seemed relics of a bygone age: white pith helmets, scarlet jackets, blue pantaloons and elongated spurs, no longer in vogue. The man who rode to the head of the procession was obviously very senior in rank and his aide a lieutenant of cavalry. When the leader reached the four nobles he drew a carbine from his holster, levelled it at the head of the nearest noble and shot him. Though Barnardo heard not a sound, the Indian slumped lifeless on his pony. Then the Englishman bumped the dead man's pony out of the way, drew a carbine from another holster and aimed it at the next man in line. It misfired when he pulled the trigger, so he threw it aside, drew his sabre and slashed the second, third and fourth Indians below the ribs with such energy that his helmet was dislodged, revealing a shock of red hair, side whiskers which were then fashionable, and a beard.

Barnardo was sickened and though his instinct was to intervene his limbs would not respond. He was puzzled by the lack of resistance on the part of any in the procession, for they could easily have slaughtered the two Englishmen.

The foul deed accomplished, the officers wheeled and rode off as fast as they could, to Delhi. The performers then broke up and joined the column, bearers came forward and draped the corpses over their ponies and secured them. The *jhilmils* of the *doolies* were closed, drums beat out a mournful throb and the chant of 'Ai! Ai! Ai!' came from thousands of throats as the procession increased its pace and turned left some 60 yards from where Barnardo stood and disappeared behind a dense mass of mahogany trees. He stood there for some minutes as the masses of troops, elephants, camels, oxen, guns and carts – the entire paraphernalia of an army – marched out of sight.

Disconcerted and wondering whether he had dreamt the entire incident, Barnardo continued till he saw the Kutab Minar, the graceful black iron column which for centuries has resisted both dust and decay.

When eventually he reached the lines of his regiment and related the details of his vision he was greeted with sceptical guffaws and told that he had been mixing his drinks. The following morning when he re-told his story at breakfast, no one laughed outright, but he could see there was polite scepticism. Two young officers agreed, however, to accompany him to the scene of his vision and five or six miles along the road to Agra they came to the spot where the procession had branched off.

'It was down there,' pointed Barnardo as he led his brother officers to the clump behind which he had sheltered. His footprints and the hoof-marks of his horse were clearly outlined, but of the procession there was not a sign. They then rode to the spot where the procession had turned left and through a gap in the trees a marble building about half the size of Buckingham Palace, was visible.

'What is that building?' asked Barnardo

'That is Humayoon's Tomb,' replied one of the officers, who had been in the district for some time. Humayoon was, of course, the famous Muslim emperor.

Barnardo had been reading Indian history and research revealed that on 22nd September 1857 when the Indian Mutiny was about to ferment, four Rajput princes had been "executed" by James Hodson, founder of the famous regiment bearing his name, on the spot where he had seen his vision. Hodson was described as having a mass of red hair and a luxuriant beard, and the officer accompanying him was Lt. Macdowell. The uniform of Hodson's Horse consisted at the time, of blue pantaloons, a scarlet jacket and a red sash, and all other details corresponded with those seen by Barnardo. Records stated that the "execution" had been carried out not far from Humayoon's Tomb.

The four young nobles had been leading their army to join the "rebels," or as they would be called today, "freedom fighters."

Barnardo's testimony cannot be brushed aside as an hallucination. He was an abstemious man who lived to be 94, a scientist by training and a Fellow of the Royal College of Surgeons. He was accustomed to sifting and weighing up evidence and even fifty years after, nothing would convince him that he had not been privileged to witness a slice of history.

Phenomena In North Carolina

Phenomena inexplicable within the bounds of natural laws have been witnessed from time to time in the mountains of North Carolina, U.S.A. In March 1951, for instance, John P. Bessor described a vision of light he had seen at Brown Mountain near Morganton, N.C., 55 miles east of Ashville on the US Route 70.

Later about 25 miles east-south-east of Ashville on US Route 74 in the famous Chimney Rock Pass where the highway cuts through a spur on the Blue Ridge, two men living near Chimney Rock Fall saw armies fight a cavalry battle in which men rode at each other, hacking and slashing with sabres; in which horses reared and fell dying, and wounded littered the Pass. Then as suddenly as it all happened the scene vanished.

Both were reliable witnesses and filed affidavits of all they had seen, at Rutherfordton Court; and during the investigation it was revealed that a cavalry action, such as that witnessed, actually took place in 1811!

ANIMALS ARE MORE PSYCHIC
THAN HUMANS

It has long been recognized that creatures nearest to Nature are more psychic than the highly civilized, on whom wind and waves; light and darkness; rain, thunder and lightning; earthquakes and other phenomena such as the aurora borealis, have far less impact. Civilized man tries to live by logic and reason, though frequently without success, whereas primitives rely on instinct* and experience.

Instinct is much stronger, even in domestic animals, than in man. Cats, for instance, will never sit in the position in which you place them but turn round and round as if making a nest, and relax only when satisfied. This may even be to see whether enemies lurk, waiting their chance to pounce. Dogs given regular meals continue to bury bones for future consumption, as they did when they hunted for food.

Animals Are Nature's Prophets

Early in December 1935 Sam Snake, Chief of the Obijway Indians and Black Hawk their tribal prophet, sent a telegram to the head of the Canadian National Railways in Toronto predicting that there would be a mild winter as geese were flying high, foxes and other fur-bearing animals had not started to don their winter coats, and the muskrat and beaver did not think that winter homes were necessary. Even fish had not taken to deep waters as they do when winters are hard and heavy frosts are expected. Black Hawk stated correctly that snowfall would be not more than a foot deep because deer had scratched the bark of trees no more than a foot from the ground and antler marks were never higher than 12 inches.

On a previous occasion Black Hawk had warned the authorities that snow would fall so thickly that it would be deep enough to bury a standing man and sure enough, Canada experienced one of the hardest winters within living memory.

*In its original sense, "animal impulse."

He had based his prediction on scratch marks made by deer, and on other signs.

Animals Know When Danger Threatens

There are countless recorded instances of animals, birds, fish and reptiles knowing that disaster was imminent when man was blissfully unaware of impending danger. For days before the great volcanic eruption on the island of Krakatoa in Indonesia in 1883, inhabitants of the surround-islands reported that the Sunda Strait was black with swimming creatures and clouds of birds winged their way inland. After the explosion, which was heard thousands of miles away, not a vestige of animal life remained on what was left of the island; nothing except the remains of some of the 36,000 people who had lived there. All wild life had been forewarned by a highly developed sixth sense.

It was also reported that shortly before the eruption of Mt. Pelee, which destroyed the town of Saint-Pierre in Martinique, and its 40,000 inhabitants, animals in the town and surrounding countryside had shown signs of panic and terror and wherever possible, had deserted their usual haunts, and birds flew off in clouds.

The Agadir Earthquake

Whereas in the past scientists dismissed such portents are nonsense they now feel that there is more than a substratum of truth in them. It was noticed that hours before the earthquake which destroyed Agadir in 1960 horses went mad in their stalls, kicked them to pieces, and those that managed to break free raced from the doomed city. The hair on dogs bristled and many leapt from windows and fled howling into the desert. Only humans slept undisturbed till the buildings crashed down on them, entombing hundreds.

We say that animals are psychic because they possess this hypersensitivity, but Professor W. N. Kellogg of Florida State University, who has conducted scores of experiments with dolphins, the results of which were published in *Science* in 1953, is convinced that their hearing is ultra-sensitive. This is undoubtedly true but they must also possess some other faculty which warns them of danger, about which we know little.

Why is it that bats can fly through a darkened room without colliding with wires and other objects; and what is it that enables homing pigeons to fly unerringly for thousands of miles without the benefit of compass and other instruments upon which man relies?

It has nothing to do with smell.

Fish Sense Danger

Fish also feel the vibrations of danger before they are perceptible to man. Japan suffers on average 1.6 earthquakes every 24 hours, few of which, fortunately, are catastrophic. They know when the crust of the earth is about to crack, even before it does so. For many years the Japanese have known that the Cat-Fish (*Parasilarus Asotus*) grow restive shortly before earthquakes, so keep specimens – ugly, whiskered creatures about three feet long – in tanks and observe them closely. If a quake is imminent the fish grow agitated, swim to the surface and try to leap out of the water; and when they find this impossible, sink to the bottom. In this way the authorities are warned of more than 80% of the earthquakes in the islands, though their exact location is never known beforehand. Even seismographs fail to record pre-earthquake tremors; fish are the only harbingers of doom.

The Loss of the S.S. Waratah

When the "S.S. Waratah" was due to sail from Durban at the turn of the century, the crew and passengers remarked on a sudden exodus of rats from the ship, all making for the shore. Old salts on board were apprehensive and predicted disaster but the Captain assured his passengers that they had nothing to fear. One passenger noticed, however, that the ship had a list of 15 degrees to port, and this coupled with the desertion of the rats, made him decide to leave the ship. Soon after she sailed and somewhere off the coast of Africa disaster overtook her and all on board were drowned. No one knows, even to this day, what became of the *Waratah*.

Cats Are Extremely Sensitive To Vibrations

We once extended our hospitality to a ginger Manx cat, for no one ever owns a cat in the same way as a dog. If I called him he invariably walked away; if we banged his plate for dinner, we would see him in the fork of a tree, watching us with one eye half closed. If I walked behind him up the garden path, hoping to pick him up, he would swivel his ears round and keep just ahead. If I bent to pick him up he would increase pace without a backward glance, keeping just out of reach. This happened so often as to convince me that he possessed some sort of inbuilt radar which informed him of my movements.

When I made journeys that took me from home for most of the day he would disappear and ignore meal times, but would come running in about five minutes before I got back, giving my wife due notice of my arrival.

Cats Often Foresee Disaster

Some say that cats are the most psychic of all domestic animals. Though this may not be true they possess a high degree of sensitivity. Captain R. S. Gwatkin-Williams, Master of the "Tara," said that when he was about to leave for Malta during one of the blackest periods of the war the ship's mascot, a black cat, grew nervous, leapt into the sea and tried to swim ashore. A boat was launched, the animal pursued, and though he fought desperately, was taken back and locked in a cabin. One can imagine the misery of the unfortunate animal who knew that disaster and death were round the corner but could not break free. A week later the "Tara" was torpedoed and sank in eight minutes. In the confusion no one thought about rescuing the poor cat.

When the "Joyita," a coaster, was about to sail from Apia in Samoa, to Mainna 20 miles away, an old tom who had made the vessel his home, suddenly grew agitated as the anchor was being weighed. Then on impulse he dashed down the gangway and vanished among the packing cases littering the wharf.

Two months later the "Joyita" was found drifting and water-logged, her crew and passengers missing. She was taken in tow, brought back and repaired, but not one of those on board was ever traced. How did the cat know?

Then there was the tabby on the "Remindo," an armed trawler engaged in hunting submarines during the first world war. She patrolled the Channel, protecting shipping between Portland and Cherbourg. The tabby was the ship's mascot and a great favourite but on 2nd February 1918 shortly before the "Remindo" sailed she grew restive and as the ship cast off and started to move, tabby rushed madly to the side, made a wild leap, landed on the wharf and dashed out of sight.

Ten minutes after casting off a violent explosion rocked the ship, which sank instantly, leaving hardly a trace and no survivors. It was impossible to deduce from the debris that floated whether she had struck a mine or been sabotaged; whatever the cause, the ship's cat had no intention of being a victim.

Another, the "Stony Point," also had a tabby which made the ship her home for nearly a year and seemed content to remain indefinitely. Then one evening just as the ship was about to put to sea she appeared on deck, her tail lashing vigorously and, as the "Stony Point" slipped her moorings, rushed to the side and made a 20-foot leap, landed on the quay and dashed away, eluding all attempts to capture her.

Not long after the "Stony Point" collided with the "Ioannis" in mid-Channel, suffering considerable damage and loss of life. The cabin and basket where the tabby slept were flooded and crushed.

Instinct – Not Smell

A Mrs. Gertrude Springer gives an example of animal instinct which saved the life of a neighbour she called Aunt Rilla. 'Do you know that we were struck by lightning? asked Aunt Rilla one evening.

'No,' said the surprised Mrs. Springer, as she awaited details; 'I did not.'

'You know I have a mongrel dog,' went on Aunt Rilla; 'whom I am very fond of. Young as he is he waits till I get to my feet before he asks to go out, and he waits outside till I'm near the door before he scratches to come in. (Aunt Rilla was injured in an accident and has trouble in getting up and down). The dog considers my condition and never makes demands when I'm seated.

'Well, on the afternoon of the storm I was reading my paper in the big chair right in front of the telephone when all of a sudden the dog began to bark and growl and make such a fuss that I couldn't heave myself out of my chair fast enough. He acted as if he had gone crazy and led me to the door when lightning struck. The bolt went right through the wires, burning them and shattering the phone and had I been in my chair I would have been killed as the wall near me was shattered, too.'

There was no suggestion of the dog smelling anything for lightning travels at more the 180,000 miles a second and the only smell it leaves is that of burning after it has struck.

Professor Ernesto Bozzano

That dogs howl at death is no mere legend, for according to Professor Ernesto Bozzano (1862–1945)* the famous Italian psychologist, considered by many to be the greatest authority on psychical research: 'The animal psyche has a mysterious faculty. Domestic animals can sometimes foresee the death of one of their household and they announce it by characteristic barking and growling.' The Germans say that goats have this faculty as well.

In his well known book on the subject, *Metaphysical Manifestations Among Animals,* Bozzano said that M. Marcel Mangin, the painter and psychiatrist, who died in 1915, had a dog that always foresaw the death of members of his family. Even before the person fell ill the dog would howl in a strange fashion, at which the family, knowing his strange power, always grew alarmed. One day the dog started to howl and as everyone seemed remarkably healthy Mangin asked: 'Whatever does he mean?'

No one seemed to know but they hadn't long to wait for next day Mangin died from an embolism.

Bozzano also cites the case of a kitten that was given to a neighbour and never tried to return. When years later its former owner died the family was surprised to see the cat, which they knew well, arrived at the door. They tried to shoo it off but it evaded them and made straight for its former master's room, where it stayed for a few minutes gazing steadfastly at him

*Italian psychologist. His *Animis and Spiritualism* is the ablest working hypothesis on the survival of the body after death

35

before it departed, never to return. How did it know he had died?

Can Your Dog Read Your Mind

Barbara Woodhouse, who understands animals better than most people says in her book *Know Your Dog* that some dogs have a deep rooted aversion to men; others hate women; and Alsatians hate either men or women instinctively if thought transference comes from an owner with a similar dislike. Dogs can sense, if not see, the auras of people, every person having an aura which gives some indication of his character and disposition.

That some animals can read the minds of their owners is also true. Hettie Chesney had many telepathic experiences with dogs in childhood. Her father owned a collie named Bruno which always responded to his thoughts. Bruno though exceedingly active, slept heavily in the dining room. Sometimes his master, in the sitting room, would think: 'Come here, Bruno,' and Bruno would invariably rise from a deep sleep and appear as if called. Chesney often performed his trick for the benefit of visitors who refused to believe that the dog would respond to mental suggestion.

One day Bruno swallowed a rubber ball and was carted off to the nearest veterinary hospital. Chesney called every day but the reports were always the same; the dog was progressing favourably. One night he rose at twelve because he could hear Bruno howling, though the hospital was more than a mile away. At one o'clock he could stand it no longer so drove to the hospital; but they refused to let him see the dog, who they said was doing well. He argued for half an hour, saying that he could hear Bruno howling but the door was closed in his face. Next morning he was informed that Bruno was dead.

But that was not the end of Bruno. He was brought home but because the ground was frozen, could not be buried. For the next few days Hettie was awakened at night by the constant rattling of Bruno's collar and leash which hung on a nail in the hall. It had been Bruno's habit to run into the hall and shake his collar when he wanted to be taken for a walk. When the ground thawed and Bruno was buried, the noise stopped. Though this may have been a coincidence, no one in the family believed it to be so.

Mia and Elephant Bill

In his book *Elephant Bill* Col. J. H. Williams gives examples of
the supernatural powers of his Alsatian, Mia. Quite by accident
he learnt that she could read his thoughts. One evening while
writing in his jungle hut in Burma, Mia grew restless and started
to prowl, breaking his concentration. 'Good heavens,' he
thought with exasperation; 'for goodness sake lie down, Mia,'
and instantly Mia lay down and remained quiet. This made him
experiment.

For a start he willed the dog to come to his side and she
obeyed. Then he left her in camp and rambled four miles, taking
an irregular route which twice crossed a river. Then he sat down
and concentrated hard on the dog, willing her to come to him.
Within an hour she was by his side!

Dr. Maurice Burton

Owners of clever dogs often say that their pets are every bit as
intelligent as humans but those who have never kept pets, or
dislike dogs, sneer at such "sickly sentimentality." Dr. Maurice
Burton, of the Natural History Museum, South Kensington,
London, however, is not so sure. He has carried out hundreds of
tests and believes that in some respects they are more intelligent
than humans. As far as the senses are concerned there is no
comparison; humans are not in the same street.

Dr. J. B. Rhine *

Dr. J. B. Rhine, of Duke University, South Carolina, USA,
perhaps the foremost living authority on ESP** carried out a
12-year study which suggests that some animals are extremely
psychic. He and Sara S. Feather, a fellow researcher, discovered
54 cases in which ESP occurred in species other than man and
checked 500 instances of "puzzling animal behaviour," which
included animals who seemed to sense the death of their masters
when far from home; impending danger to the masters or their

*Duke was the first university to establish a department of parapsychology, with Rhine
as its head.

**Extra-sensory-perception

pets; or imminent dangers to masters before they set out on journeys. His study described 54 cases in which a pet dog, cat or bird followed a departed master 'into wholly unfamiliar territory at a time and under conditions which allow the use of no conceivable sensory trail.' From this he concluded that 'animals would have to be regarded by a still unrecognized means of knowing,' to perform such feats.

The Sense That Huskies Possess

In huskies, which are half-dog, half-wolf, this faculty has been developed to an extraordinary degree and there are innumerable instances where the leader of a pack has led a team to safety through uncharted country.

Huskies are incredibly tough. According to Scotty Allan, one of the greatest dog mushers of all time, they can sleep out in temperatures of 80 degrees below zero, when a team will huddle together for warmth, and live on frozen fish for months. They nuzzle in the snow for water and gnaw rawhide for food, and they 'can tear off 100 miles between dawn and dusk.'

Sir Wilfred Grenfell recalled that on one occasion he had to travel 70 miles over strange country which no one had travelled that winter and the trail was uncut and unblazed. The leading dog had, however, been over the trail the previous winter when the going was terribly difficult. There had been fog, it has snowed heavily, and the journey had taken three days. Much of the route led over frozen lakes and through woods but Grenfell had complete trust in the leader who piloted them to safety to their destination without pause or error, in 12 hours, including stops for food, of 1½ hours. He could not possibly have followed a scent as blizzards had covered the trail during the past 12 months.

Animals Have a Homing Instinct

Take a human being to a strange place on a cloudy day and he will have no idea in which direction home lies; if he is in the desert he will walk round in circles. All animals, however, have a homing instinct which is stronger in some than in others. The Scorano family who lived in Turin owned an Alsatian named

Lassie, after the animal made famous by films. She loved playing with the children, but Pancrazio Scorano felt that the city was no place for a large active dog so took her to Brindizi in the south, there to live with relatives.

But Lassie loved her family too much to remain contented and soon after the Scoranos returned they had a phone call to say that Lassie had vanished. So Signor Scorano boarded the next train to Brindizi and searched for a week without finding her. He got back to find his children heart broken and each night they prayed fervently for her return. A month later they moved to another part of Turin, but their prayers did not abate.

Then a week later the tenant of their old home phoned to say: 'There is an Alsatian here. I am sure she is your Lassie.' Scorano was there with the speed of light. He found Lassie exhausted, with bleeding paws, her tail wagging feebly with pleasure as he embraced her. She had walked more than 700 miles over difficult country, had crossed the rugged Appenines which run down the spine of Italy, had swum rivers, negotiated busy road and railway lines to get back to her beloved family. Needless to say, they were never parted again. But how did she know in which direction to set her course and how far to go?

Cats are not renowned for their walking ability, yet Sooty, a black tom, who was taken by the Hannams when they moved from Egham in Surrey to Hartlepool in Durham, found he could not settle in the barbarous North and decided to return to his former haunts. After two weeks he felt he had had enough and vanished, walking 300 miles back to his former "home."

Nor are ducks made for walking, so Mrs. Charlton Chapman of Gunton, Suffolk, who sold one of her ducks to a farmer three miles away, was astonished next morning to see it waddling wearily up the garden path. Obviously, it must have been homesick and pining for its mistress.

Even alligators seem to know where they belong, for when Mr. L. B. Jolly who farmed at Great Buckland, Cobham, Kent, sent a pet alligator he kept in a wired-in pond to a zoo eight miles away, he was astonished *next morning* to see it trying to get through the wire netting to its pond!

St. Bernards

Certain breeds of dogs are more psychic than others. St.

Bernards, for instance, which are maintained by the Swiss authorities to rescue climbers and tourists trapped by avalanches, are almost clairvoyant. Ferdinand Schmutz, a civil servant who later became Superintendent of the National Library in Berne, has written widely about these dogs in articles and in his lavishly illustrated book, *My Dog*. One of the stories he tells is of a rescue just before the Second World War, involving a dog named Moritz. When reports came in that 15 skiers were buried in an avalanche near Murren, a rescue party was hurried to the scene where they managed to dig through and haul out 14 members of the party. They had given up hope of finding the last man when Moritz, who was not a St. Bernard but a mongrel, began to bark and scratch furiously in the snow.

When ordered to desist he ignored the command and continued to rake with his hind legs. As the spot was some distance to that in which the others had been found the rescuers dug there only with reluctance and eventually came across the last skier. Moritz couldn't possibly have smelt him; his agitation was caused by a sense of danger which made him continue scratching.

Later as an experiment Schmutz had a hole dug, asked some volunteers to lie in it and covered them with snow. Then he took Moritz to the spot but after sniffing around for a few seconds he took himself off. Obviously he knew there was no danger; he could sense where danger existed and it was this that gave Schmutz the idea of training dogs for patrol, messenger and Red Cross work. Their sixth sense tells them unerringly when danger is present.

The Psychic Cat

Cats possess senses which humans lack. One known to K. C. Liddell of Winscombe, Somerset, possessed this faculty. He wrote of an experience during the 1914–18 war. 'As I was born in Shanghai and spent my formative years in China I was given command of a Chinese labour force in Etaples, Northern France, during the war.

'I was responsible for their welfare and understood their mentality, which helped to convince them that the warnings of air raids by a stray black cat were worth taking seriously.

'We had no official warning of air raids and had to rely on our hearing to take shelter. Sometimes this gave us little or no time. The cat of which I write would come into my hut a considerable period before the enemy planes came over and waken me up! This happened so regularly that the minute it appeared I mustered the men and we all took shelter in good time. I am sure that this cat saved many lives – including mine. I am not what is known as a cat lover, no doubt being a little afraid of their super-intelligence, but I live to bless this one.'

Bloodhounds

For tracking purposes bloodhounds are the most extraordinary of all dogs. Captain V. G. Mullikin, one of the most famous bloodhound men in America, believed that they followed not only the scent on the ground but where this was impossible, for instance over water, they followed the aura of the person they were tracking. They would lift their muzzles high and stand as it were on tiptoe to sniff the breeze if the scent on the earth was lost. The best time for tracking is a cool damp night when the aura is undisturbed, and the worst a hot dry day when a strong wind is blowing, which reinforces his theory.

THE SIXTH SENSE

The normal person has five senses: sight, hearing, smell, taste and touch. Before man became civilized it was probable that he possessed a sixth sense which warned of impending danger from enemies or natural catastrophes. There is no accounting for this sense; no logical explanation. One just feels and acts accordingly.

As men grew civilized and started to live in brick and concrete homes, often far from natural surroundings, this sense was gradually lost, till today comparatively few possess it to a practical degree. Those who are subject to a sixth sense are said to have premonitions which the psychologists define as 'Thoughts, usually accompanied by anxiety, of a coming event, derived from some experience or suggestion, which may be irrelevant, but is regarded as a warning; in psychical research the use of word implies a revelation from supernormal sources.'

In practice, however, a premonition may not be derived from some experience or suggestion; it may be atavistic; that is, the reappearance of a character which has not shown itself for generations. This suggests that events which occurred in the dim past to three or four generations of ancestors, may still have some impact on one. We may still live in the shadow of those who have gone before though we may not have the remotest connection with, or knowledge of them. Heredity therefore dogs one and all and is something from which none can escape.

Though most people are not psychic nearly everyone harbours some secret atavistic fear which constantly makes them look over their shoulders; a feeling that disaster in a specific form will some day overtake them.

There is no logical explanation for such feelings and no matter how brave a face one presents to the world, these secret fears persist and the only way one can banish them is by psychiatry, which may be a lengthy process, or through hypnosis, which takes one back in time, unearths the fear or fears, and dissipates them.

The Case of William Terriss

Will Terriss, the famous actor, who was known to be courageous, had a horror of cold steel. When offered the part of Marat which would have suited him admirably as a character actor, to the surprise of all he turned it down because after reading the play he found it impossible to play the last scene, in which the demogogue was stabbed by Charlotte Corday. Throughout his life Terriss had a premonition that he would be stabbed to death and he was not going to risk this happening, even in a play with a "trick" knife. He felt that one night the knife would fail to work and he would die.

His sixth sense happened to be a true guide for one evening in 1897 as he was leaving the Adelphi theatre, a mentally deranged person who nurtured an imaginary grudge, plunged a knife through his breast bone, killing him.

Although not psychic or even sensitive, there are many who on occasions have had premonitions which enabled them to avoid death or disaster, or have business dealings with associates who intend to swindle them. A premonition may happen only once in a lifetime but more often than not when confided to a friend or relative it is dismissed with scorn, sometimes to the subject's regret.

There is no accounting for premonitions. Often they enter the mind suddenly; sometimes they simmer and develop for weeks or months. Frances Davis, a Master of Science who made a reputation writing sociological articles, described an incident in which her brother was involved. He farmed in Pennsylvania and one warm day while driving over the mountains he started feeling stiff, so decided to park, stretch his legs and have an *al fresco* lunch. Finding a pleasant spot on a ridge overlooking a lovely view, he sat down with a flask of coffee beside him and began to unpack his sandwiches.

Then for no reason he could possibly advance he felt that a rattlesnake was behind him and about to attack. Yet the only snakes he had ever seen were in a zoo, among them a rattler. The premonition was so sudden and powerful that instantly he tensed his leg muscles and bounded forward as far as he could before turning. Behind and within striking distance of his seat was the biggest rattler imaginable, drawing itself back as if to strike. Then came the rustle of leaves, the typical rattling whir, but by that time he was well out of range and making for his cab. Why had he suddenly felt that this venomous reptile was behind him, for there is nothing to indicate its presence?

One meaning of the word "monition" is "warning," and is

derived from the Latin *monere* or call to mind. A premonition is a silent warning which comes to one before a risk is taken or a danger encountered. Premonitions are always accompanied by feelings of apprehension, which in most cases make one feel uneasy but are usually brushed off as the result of over-indulgence. In a few instances it is so strong and frightening that in spite of all logic, action has to be taken.

Sir Richard Gale

General Sir Richard Gale, formerly CIGS and later head of the NATO armed forces,* commanded a company during the First World War. At one stage he was ordered to take over a section of the line from a New Zealand battalion. The shelling was heavy and one of his officers named Taylor confided to him: 'I'm sure I'm not going to come out of this show alive. I feel it in my bones.' Gale assured him he had no more to fear than the rest of them and tried to laugh him out of his despondency.

That night, however, when Gale was leading his company through a forest a long range, high velocity shell whistled over their heads and burst about a hundred yards behind. The shells arrived at such a speed that though one could hear them they seldom allowed time for evasion. One just heard them whizz – and then came the explosion.

'I had an uncomfortable feeling,' recalled Gale; 'that the next one would drop on us – and sure enough, it did.'

Though it was a black night and the rain was coming down in rods he went back to find out what damage had been done. 'Only one man's been hit,' a sergeant who had counted the men, told him.

'Who is he?' asked Gale, though instinctively he knew.

'Lieutenant Taylor, sir.'

His sixth sense had told Taylor that his time had come and, because he like the others, had to obey orders, he accepted his fate stoically. As there was nothing he could have done to escape his fate why did he have this premonition?

Call To Arms: Sir Richard Gale

44

David Herbert Knew

David Herbert, mentioned earlier, served as a radio operator in the Merchant Navy during the Second World War. He was a sensitive person and in December 1943 knew instinctively that his vessel would be torpedoed on the next voyage. As he had been on a number of trips during the past two years this was strange; but as the feeling grew more powerful with each day of his leave that he packed all the possessions he valued in his cabin – pictures, books, furniture and gramophone – and took them back to Wilton, his ancestral home.

Then a few days after Christmas they sailed for Algiers. He was sitting in his cabin taking middle watch as they wallowed in the Bay of Biscay when a torpedo hit them amidships. The vessel foundered and many of the crew lost their lives in the rough sea.

Colonel Jim Corbett

Most men who live in the wilds develop a sixth sense which warns them of danger and Colonel Jim Corbett,* famous for his adventures with tigers in Northern India, developed his to an uncanny degree, for he spent most of his days next to Nature. Often for no apparent reason he would feel that danger was lurking round the corner and although vigilance had become second nature to him, would take extra precautions. One day he had a premonition that a man-eating leopard – a much craftier beast than a tiger – lay waiting, crouched behind a huge rock. He paused and then decided to make a detour and emerge on the other side of the rock. It was fortunate that he did so for sure enough, perched on a ledge was the crouching leopard, waiting to pounce as he passed. It would have torn him to shreds before he could have raised his rifle. As it happened, the animal was so absorbed that he was able to dispatch it with a single bullet.

Incidentally, Corbett was not one of those "sportsmen" who killed tigers and leopards for their skins, or to boast about the numbers that had fallen to their marksmanship; he went after them only when villagers reported that they had killed cattle and carried off men and women, for contrary to the general belief

*Man Eaters of Kumaon: Jim Corbett

tigers do not normally attack people. They do so only when circumstances make it imperative and many a tiger passed without any attempt to molest him.

The Extraordinary Case of Ten-Year Old Horst

In 1953 an extraordinary case of sixth sense set the entire city of Munich talking. A class in one of the schools was given the task of writing an essay on one of the following subjects: (1) The Place of My Birth (2) My Mother (3) A Fatal Traffic Accident (4) On The Road (5) An attractive Profession For A Woman.

A lad named Horst chose the third and described in exact detail how a young cyclist in a hurry to get home tried to pass a lorry laden with tiles, and as he was about to overtake the truck it swerved and threw him from his machine. The boy was taken to hospital but was dead on arrival.

An hour later Horst left school, mounted his bike and rode off. On the way he tried to pass a heavily laden lorry – with tiles – though he did not know that it carried. As he was level with the lorry it swerved, throwing him to the pavement on which he struck his head. Everything happened as described in his essay. It could all be put down to coincidence but as each detail tallied with those in his essay it seemed that Horst must have had a premonition. In any case, it gave the newspapers an excellent story.

Alexander Skirving

In 1850 Alexander Skirving, a master mason, worked for the well known firm of Mowlem, Burt and Freeman, which held a contract for all government work in London. One morning at ten while working on the gate at the north-east corner of Regent's Park, east of the Zoo, he felt an overpowering impulse to return home, which was so far from Regent's Park that he had brought a packed lunch with him.

For some time he tried to brush off the feeling that something was wrong but eventually it grew so strong that even the thought that he would lose 6d an hour – a considerable sum for a working man at the time – did not deter him. After half an hour of wrestling with himself he packed up. Another hour of fast walking brought him to his door where he was greeted by his sister-in-law, a Mrs. Vyse, who lived nearby.

'Why Alex,' she cried in amazement; 'how did you know?'

'Know what?' he asked.

'Why, about Mary Ann.'

'I don't know anything about Mary Ann,' he confessed, growing more anxious every second.

'Then what brought you home?'

'I can hardly tell you. I seemed to want to come – as if I was needed. What's wrong?'

Mrs. Vyse then told him that his wife had been run down by a cab about an hour and a half earlier; the very instant he had been assailed by his premonition, and had called for him incessantly as the doctor and nurse were tending her. He hurried upstairs where his wife, looking weak and ill, held out her hands to him. He took them in his, at which she fell asleep. From that moment her condition improved. 'The crisis is past,' the doctor told him; 'but I don't think she would have recovered had you not arrived just then.'

It is probable that Skirving's premonition was caused by sympathetic waves sent out by his wife and conducted through the ether, and the reason he had received them is that they were very close to each other. There are some who have such a strong affinity with each other that their thoughts can be transposed.

The Strange Case of Mitzi Ryan

This may also have been so in the case of Peter Ryan, a carpenter, who lived in a flat in south-east London, with his wife Mitzi. After ten months both looked forward to the birth of their first child, for they were very much in love with each other.

Early in their marriage, however, both had premonitions of tragedy which visited them in the form of nightmares. Peter dreamed night after night that Mitzi would suddenly die. A few days later he had the same dream, even more vividly.

Then Mitzi dreamt that tragedy was just around the corner, which frightened her. 'I always felt that we were just too happy for it to be true,' she said. 'I know it sounds silly but life really was a honeymoon for Peter and me.'

Night after night her dreams recurred. Always the same dream. 'I could see Pete falling. One minute he would be on a boat; then he would suddenly fall overboard. I could see water everywhere and I could see Pete under the water, his arms

47

waving in the air. I never saw him again but I knew he was dead.'

The dreams were all the more terrifying because a friend had just built a boat and wanted Peter to sail with him, but Mitzi begged him not to go.

At the time their bank account was in the red and Peter was so worried that he had an insurance policy made out on Mitzi transferred to him. Which was fortunate because days after he had a fall at work and was found lying in a pool of water. They rushed him to hospital but life had expired.

While in hospital a Mr. West was brought in with a failing heart and after he died Mitzi asked if his heart could be transplanted to Pete's body. Mrs. West agreed and though the operation was a success Pete did not respond as well as expected. 'There is one thing I can tell Mrs. West,' said Mitzi after the operation; his heart couldn't have been put into a better body.' Incidentally, it was the first heart transplant to take place in Britain and was fully reported in the national newspapers.*

Dr. Rhine's Experiments

Dr. J. B. Rhine has tried for years, so far unsuccessfully, to find out exactly what ESP is. He and his colleagues have proved its existence but the nearest definition he can give is: 'ESP is a general process of which telepathy and clairvoyance are special forms,' and that those who have a highly developed sixth sense are usually both telepathic and clairvoyant. Sometimes drugs, narcotics and stimulants enable people to develop ESP temporarily though the continued use of such agents undermines the system because they are habit forming and destroys those addicted to their use.

There is no connection between a sixth sense and intelligence for simetimes retarded children possess ESP to a remarkable degree.

According to Dr. Rhine retarded children frequently scored higher marks during tests with zener** cards than the most brilliant scholars. The most remarkable of his conclusions was that people showed a marked aptitude for a year or two after

*People: 9.6.1968

**Zener cards: named after their inventor. Five cards bearing simple diagrams. A pack consists of 50 with 10 of each kind.

which their ability to guess correctly declined; and this, possibly, happens to all who possess ESP – clairvoyants, etc. It may also account for the fact that people who have premonitions have them occasionally, or only once in a lifetime, and never again. The sixth sense is not a gift that the normal person can develop at will though yogis claim that by practising *asanas* (special exercises), *pranayama* (yoga breathing) and their way of life, intuition and perception which are part of ESP, can be developed. They also claim that such practices enable them to levitate and cause the astral body to leave the physical body and take extensive journeys.

Some persons are intuitive and others are not.

Storehouse Of The Brain

Science has established that the average human brain weighs 1,300 grammes or about 3 lb, though the size of the brain varies enormously and has no connection with intellect. Anatole France, the author, had a brain weighing no more than 39 oz, and Gambetta, the French stateman, 41 oz; whereas Cromwell and Byron each had brains weighing 781/2 oz. Shelley the poet; Descartes the philosopher and mathematician; Donizetti the operatic composer; and Schumann the pianist and composer, all had brains of less than normal weight.

Your brain stores everything you have ever heard, seen, touched, tasted and smelt, thought or experienced. Under hypnosis the subconscious can be explored and you can be made to recall the day of the week on which your fourth birthday fell, the name of the doctor who treated you for measles, when you passed your first examination or kicked your first goal at football, and a million other trifling events and incidents now relegated to the limbo of the past.

Under certain conditions some of these events may come to light in a jumbled form in dreams, but rarely as sharply and as accurately as under hypnosis because the conscious mind is asleep. When the conscious mind is awake it responds to reason; what we lack is the key that will enable us to make a mental switch by turning on intuition at will. Intuition is something more than animal instinct and experiments have shown that it is most powerful in warm, intelligent people, and more usual in women than in men. Intuition is linked with inspiration, which must come of its own accord and cannot be forced. Both are locked in the vaults of the subconscious.

Intuition and Inspiration

Some years ago 253 writers, artists and musicians in America were questioned about the mind processes in their work and 75% stated that intuition played a major part in creation.

'A man may think he reasons with cold logic,' said Dr. Willis R. Whitney, the noted inventor; 'actually he reaches the solution through a hunch and works out the reasons afterwards.'

Pasteur said: 'Intuition is given only to he who has undergone long preparation to receive it,' and this is true of the medical profession, for the old family doctor often said he could "smell" typhoid and other diseases.

Intuition and inspiration often work in normal everyday affairs for those who have stored away information by study and hard labour, and the saying that 'inspiration is 90% perspiration' is true. When Edison had a particularly tough problem to unravel he would prime himself with all the available facts, think his immediate problem through and then let his mind simmer. Suddenly, when he was *not* thinking of the problem, for no apparent reason the solution would appear out of the blue.

One day a high executive complained to John D. Rockefeller about his salary and said that one of his colleagues who did nothing but gaze out of his window received 50,000 dollars a year. 'I think it's grossly unfair,' he said indignantly.

Rockefeller pondered for a moment. 'If you look out of the window and think the kind of thoughts he is thinking, I'll pay you 50,000 dollars, too.'

Everyone knows that authors, poets and musicians are subject to fits of inspiration, which are the results of concentrated thought about characters and plots. Thoughts must have some meat on which to chew. But not many realize that scientists, engineers and inventors are sometimes inspired when they "chew" over apparently insurmountable problems.

Marcel Breuer

Marcel Breuer, who invented tubular steel furniture, was in the Bauhaus in Dessau in 1925 devoting most of his time to thinking

50

of ways to improve the design of wooden furniture and make it more economical and durable. One day he bought a bicycle and not knowing how to ride, set out to learn. He kept staring at the handle-bars as he strained and struggled and tried to keep his balance. Then suddenly he stopped thinking about riding and fell to the ground for the idea of making furniture from tubes, like the handle-bars, flashed into his mind. It also made a fortune for him.*

Schrodinger had been pondering over mathematical problems till his brain was tired, so he decided on a holiday to rest. As he sat in the train thinking of nothing in particular all his study and thought bore fruit. He was looking out of the window at the fields as they sped by when the pieces of the jig-saw fell into place and he had invented his wave-mechanics.

Problems Solved By Inspiration

Harry Fergusson, whose tractor is used by farmers the world over, was an insomniac. As he couldn't sleep he used to read light fiction in bed to pass the hours. He said that it was during such periods, when his mind was completely switched off from work that many of the ideas floated into his brain; solving problems which had proved insuperable when he had been working on them.**

Claude Hill was another. While Technical Director of Aston Martin he had tried for months to solve the problem of constant four wheel drive through a controlled differential, the toughest nut he had ever tried to crack. One night utterly defeated, he decided not to allow the problem to worry him, laid his head on his pillow and went to sleep. At about three o'clock he woke with a start with the key to his problem clear in his mind. The only paper on his bedside table was a copy of the "Evening Standard," so he seized a pencil and made a rapid rudimentaty sketch in the stop press column. Then with a sigh of relief he slept soundly till morning. He made an elaborate drawing, filling in details, and presented it to Tony Rolt, the racing driver and one of the firm's technical experts, when he reached the works. Both agreed that the problem had been solved and, when it was tried out, worked perfectly.

*Fifty years with science: J. G. Crowther

**Harry Fergusson: Colin Fraser

Mathematical Problems

Mathematical problems have also been solved by flashes of inspiration when those working on them were resting or engaged in different work, or in pleasure. The chemist Kekule who was working on the origin of the theory of molecular structure, decided to call it a day and return home to Clapham. 'One fine evening,' he says; 'I was returning home by the last omnibus, outside, as usual, through the deserted streets of the metropolis, which at other times was full of life. I fell into a reverie, and lo, the atoms were gambolling before my eyes!'

Henry Poincare

Henry Poincare, one of the greatest modern mathematicians, had come up against a dead wall on the work he was doing, and decided to take a day off and make up a party on a geologic expedition. 'The incidents of the travel made me forget my mathematical work,' he said;' and having reached Coutances, we entered an omnibus to go to some place or other. At the moment when I put my foot on the step, the idea came to me, without anything in my former thoughts seeming to pave the way for it, that the transformations I had used to define the Fuchsian functions were identical with those of non-Euclidian geometry. I did not verify the idea; I should not have had the time as, on taking my seat in the omnibus, I went on with a conversation already commenced, but I felt a perfect certainty. On my return to Caen, for conscience sake, I verified the result at my leisure.' In the fleeting moment, when his mind was engaged in anything but his work, by some unfathomable means, an idea had been released by his subconscious, enabling him to solve a problem that had baffled mathematicians and which only a handful of people on earth knew anything about.*

Scientists and Inventors

Scientists and inventors sometimes get their most brilliant ideas while engaged in activities far removed from their work. Nikola Tesla, a more far seeing and cleverer inventor than Edison, had

*A Signpost of Mathematics: A. H. Read

ideas which others, and Edison, thought were impracticable. One was the invention of the induction coil; the other that of alternating current, which Edison said was impossible. Tesla was watching a sunset and recalling a poem by Goethe when he realized the possibility of alternating current and at once set about putting it into practice. George Westinghouse gave him 1,000,000 dollars – then an immense sum – plus 10% of all rights, for his invention.*

Alfred Williams

During the Second World War depth charges caused innumerable problems for submarine commanders; one was the cracking of electric batteries, which emitted poisonous fumes, making life unbearable in an enclosed space. Alfred Williams, an engineer working for the Admiralty, set his mind on inventing a medium that would stand up to the battering they received when depth charges were exploded in the vicinity. Some were forced to the surface and sunk and losses were having a serious effect on the war. During 1941 Williams concentrated so hard and long on the problem that he could not sleep and the skin round his scalp tightened. Eventually he found it difficult to think clearly and began to lose his power of speech. Then, one October morning when he *wasn't thinking of the problem* the perfect idea for an unbreakable battery came to him in a flash and the taut skin on his forehead burst and blood covered his face. His wife did all she could to prevent him going to the office but he had to work out his ideas otherwise they might have vanished. Within the next few hours he made sketches, rough calculations and collected the material for a new type of battery, which resisted all explosions except direct hits. The scar on his forehead, however, caused by the bursting of skin, remained as a life-long reminder of his long mental effort.* life-long reminder of his long mental effort.**

Inspiration and ideas come to those who have acquired knowledge, and concentration brings them to fruition during periods of rest. This seldom happens to the ignorant or the lazy whose minds have nothing to work on.

The Prodigal Genius: J. J. O'Neill
**The Devices of War:* Norman Kemp

53

Freud On Hunches

Though we cannot produce scientific reasons for hunches, they should never be dismissed as rubbish. Freud once put it like this: 'When making a decision of minor importance, I have always found it advantageous to consider all the pros and cons. In vital matters, however, such as the choice of a mate or a profession, the decision should come from the unconscious, from somewhere within ourselves . . .'

That is why parents are so often mistaken when they decide "what is good" for their sons and daughters and by a process of logic determine the most suitable spouses or professions. In almost every instance the instinctive, intuitive choice of a boy or girl is better than that of a parent, for Nature mates by instinct and not by choice. And one is guided towards a profession by inclination and not by reason.

Intuition works in everyday affairs and is usually a sound guide, especially where women are concerned, as women are more intuitive than men.

A Feeling Saved His Life

Though allied in some way to intuition, a premonition is not quite the same. That hunches have saved many a life, is true. On 9th January 1968 Leslie Hockenhull, the second man on the footplate of the Manchester-London express would normally have remained in his cab till he was relieved at Stoke-on-Trent. That day, however, he broke a long standing habit and went back to the seventh coach because he had a premonition that the train would crash. Sure enough, at 12.29 p.m. the train, travelling at 80 mph, hit a transporter on an unmanned crossing at Hixon while Hockenhull was discussing summer holidays with a woman passenger. His three mates in the cab were killed.

During the inquiry which followed, he told the panel: 'Ninety nine times out of a hundred I would have stayed in the cab. I don't know what made me leave. It was just a feeling I had inside me.' Had he conveyed his feeling to his mates they would have laughed and called him a superstitious old woman.

Dennis Clowes Knew He Would Die

Dennis Clowes of Gawsworth, Macclesfield, was a wealthy cattle dealer. In January 1968 he decided to take his family to Las Palmas for a month's holiday to break up the dreary north country winter. In 1963 the family had decided to take a Christmas cruise but just missed catching the "Lakonia," which was fortunate, as the vessel caught fire in mid-Atlantic and went down with the loss of 128 lives.

In 1968 17-year old John Clowes and his brother Dennis were unable at the last moment to make the trip as John was detained in hospital with cuts, and Dennis with a foot injury. So their parents set off alone. A day or two earlier Clowes, snr., normally a jovial man who loved a joke and a laugh, seemed abnormally depressed and spoke about a fear he had of being killed. Mrs. Lily Payne, his secretary, said later: 'On the eve of his holiday Mr. Clowes was in a strange mood. Usually he was lively and gay but on this occasion he seemed subdued and was worried.

'He gave me the impression he had had a premonition something was going to happen. He asked me what I would do if anything went wrong on his holiday. He said he wanted to know what would happen to his business if he had an accident and did not come back. I think he firmly believed he could sense impending disaster.'

On 9th January he and his wife boarded the train on which Leslie Hockenhull was a member of the engine crew, and when the train crashed Mr. and Mrs. Clowes were killed. If only he had taken notice of his hunch both might have been alive today; but in similar circumstances how many would be swayed by a similar feeling? Most people would have put it down to indigestion.

Voice That Saved His Life

Premonitions come in all sorts of curious ways; at times through irresistible urges, through voices or in ghostly forms. Mr. J. C. H. Wheeler of Bromley, Kent, said: 'While working as a Superintendent of Police in Central India a few years ago I climbed a tree at a water hole to shoot a large and ferocious leopard. It was the hottest time of the year and we were expecting the monsoons to break. My companion, an Indian hunter, had a dry cough, so I told him to wait 50 yards away.

Large raindrops began to fall and I was suddenly aware of a voice from a nearby tree about 30 yards away. It called to me: "Come here quickly, sir." My thoughts were on bagging the leopard so I scrambled down one tree and up the other.

'Before I had time to make myself comfortable the tree on which I had just been seated was struck by lightning and crashed into the water hole. The Indian hunter came running expecting to find me dead. The "ghost" voice had saved my life,' for when I told him of the voice he swore he hadn't called.

A ghost voice also saved the life of Gawaine Hamilton of Kensington, London, who wrote to a newspaper: 'Before the war a friend in whose company I used to spend much time was in the habit of smoking cigars. Almost invariably when we met he drew his cigar case from his pocket, offered it to me then, with a chuckle say: 'No, they'd only make you sick.' He was killed at Dunkirk in 1940.

'In the Italian campaign I took over a billet formerly occupied by the enemy. On the table lay an apparently unopened box of cigars. As I stretched my hand towards it I "heard" the once familiar taunting chuckle and my friend's voice saying: 'No, they'd only make you sick.' I did not touch the box and subsequent examination revealed it to be a booby trap.

Lord Ebbisham's Escape

Premonitions in the form of feelings are the most common warnings. A Mr. A. W. Green of Cheshunt said: 'Late one drizzling night in the winter of 1927 I was driving a solid-tyred bus up the deserted City Road in the direction of Old Street. As I approached the gates of the HAC Barracks I suddenly felt a sensation of dread. It was so strong that in something like a panic I stopped the bus quickly about 15 yards from the gates. The bus skidded to the kerb violently and my conductor was thrown to the floor.

'As I was trying to find some convincing reply to his questions a carriage drawn by four horses came out of the barrack gates. It was one of the City ceremonial landaus and inside was the Lord Mayor (Sir Rowland Blades, later Lord Ebbisham) himself. Had I not had a presentiment of danger my bus would have hit the landau square amidships, killing or injuring the Lord Mayor.'

Though one should not be panicked by every feeling of danger experienced, there are occasions when premonitions are almost irresistibly strong and should be acted upon. Just such a premonition came to Mr. W. H. Spencer, the driver of a fast goods train in 1930. 'One night,' he relates; 'we were thundering down a long gradient into a two-mile tunnel. I had an unaccountable feeling that something would happen as we swept into the tunnel. My hand unconsciously tightened on the regulator and I glanced at my mate. I peered ahead and being somewhat reassured by green lights twinkling in the distance, opened the throttle another trifle.

'We were speeding between the rocky walls of the cutting and a moment later roared into the tunnel. Then the feeling returned and, breaking into a clammy sweat, I shut off steam, applied the vacuum brake and frantically twisted the hand brake.

'The heavy train was nearly halfway through the tunnel when it ground to a stop and I mopped my brow. Round the bend bobbed the lighted lamp carried by the guard of a passenger train which had stopped inside the tunnel with a broken axle. My uncanny premonition had prevented a ghastly accident.'

Harry Carr – The Queen's Jockey

Strong premonitions are often accompanied by a feeling of panic. In 1962 Harry Carr, the Queen's Jockey, had a powerful feeling that disaster would overtake him in the Derby. 'I know that there is going to be trouble here today,' he told his trainer; 'and it will be dangerous. I want to keep away from it if I can and I'll be happy if I'm drawn about nineteenth.'

Carr was riding Hethersett, the favourite, and trouble started just past the mile post when a bunch of leading riders began to fight for position. 'Those inside,' said Bill Rickaby, a jockey; 'were fighting to get out and those outside were fighting to get in. I could see something terrible was going to happen.'

Then, about six furlongs from the post Romulus ridden by Swinburne, hit the heels of Crossen ridden by Larraun, and both went down. Romulus fell awkwardly to the right and Hethersett crashed into him, and with him several thousands of pounds in bets.

Behind Hethersett came King Canute ridden by Lewis; Changing Times by Gosling; and Persian Fantasy by Smith. And the lot fell on Hethersett! On top of the heap piled Pindaric ridden by 21-year old Bobby Elliott, riding his first Derby. Luckily he escaped injury. Close behind was Neville Sellwood on Larkspur at 22–1, who kept his head, spurred Larkspur into a flying leap over Hethersett, guided him expertly through the mêlée and ran on to victory.

When Harry Carr woke up in hospital his first question was: 'How much did I win by?' He had suffered a fractured collar bone, a spinal injury and severe concussion.

Carr, who was expecting trouble the whole way made a supreme effort to avoid Romulus, but Romulus had fallen so awkwardly that Hethersett had no chance. This was an instance in which though warned, the subject could not possibly have avoided disaster. The only way Carr could have done so was to have scratched from the race but, as the Queen's jockey such a course was unthinkable.

Hamish McArthur's Mother

In 1958 Hamish McArthur, head of the Development Division of the Iron and Steel Board in London and a prominent member of the Alpine Club, decided to go on an expedition to North-West India in the Hindu Kush Mountains. Approval had been given by the Royal Geographical Society and assistance was offered by the Mount Everest Foundation.

About a month before he left, his mother, who always paid him an annual visit in September, became convinced she would never see him once he left England, so travelled down to his home in Richmond in June. This was strange as he was a careful, resourceful climber not given to taking risks and one of the best mountaineers in the game. Moreover, this was his third expedition to the Himalayas.

His mother did nothing to deter him for she knew that his hobby was a dangerous one and in any case, no matter what she said, it would have made no difference. Even so, nothing would shake her conviction that she had seen the last of him when they said good-bye. So she was not in the least bit surprised when at the end of July his wife received a cable to say that he had fallen to his death. Why then, had a premonition come to her?

Saved From The Nazis

'In December 1938,' wrote Miss Joan Barker of Gipsy Hill, London; 'while touring through France, circumstances compelled me to remain for some weeks in Chalon-sur-Saône, where I was invited by some wealthy people to give a talk on Britain to a society ostensibly formed to further friendly relations between the nations through the medium of languages.

'My hosts were charming and their hospitality without stint. I was invited to come again the following evening. But during the night I was so obsessed by a feeling of dread that I left the town on the following morning, giving no excuse.

'In December 1939 I read in the newspapers that my hosts had been arrested by the French police as Nazi agents on the night I should have visited them.' Had Miss Barker accepted their invitation she, too, would have been seized, because many of these so-called friendly associations were set up by the Nazis to brain-wash unsuspecting people, implicate them and turn them into allies or agents.

The Girl Who Changed Her Mind

To change her mind is a woman's prerogative; and Miss Gina Beauchamp is alive today because she did just that. She and her mother, who lived in Birkenhead, were going on holiday to Perpignan, France, but as they travelled by coach to Manston Airport in Kent, Miss Beauchamp became uneasy and as mile after mile reeled off the feeling grew worse. On reaching Manston it became an obsession. 'I know,' she cried; ' that if I fly today the plane will crash and I shall be killed.' Her mother tried her utmost to persuade her that nothing would happen but she was so distraught that there was no course other than to leave her behind while her mother flew on.

In 1967 fifteen planes landed each night at Perpignan, most of them packed with tourists bound for the Costa Brava and though the airport is surrounded by a ring of mountains no pilot had ever crashed. That night, however, a DC-4 operated by Air Ferry was not so lucky. A wing touched a rock face, the plane crashed in a blazing mass and all on board, including Mrs. Beauchamp, were killed.

Mrs. Beauchamp would have been saved had she heeded her daughter's warning but she could not bring herself to believe there was anything in her presentiment.

The Strange Case of Reg Nelms

Reg Nelms had a peculiar "gift," if one could term it as such. During the 1939–45 war he served with Bomber Command and sometimes before a trip he seemed preoccupied. If his wife asked him what was wrong he would say that some of the crew in his plane would not be coming back, and he would name them. He was always right, but kept the information to himself.

In 1944 at the end of a spell of leave he was transferred to Coastal Command for the U-boats had become such a menace that Britain was in danger of being starved into submission. Nelms was given command of a Liberator and detailed to patrol an area halfway between the Lofoten Islands and Jan Mayen Island, about 1,000 miles from Tain.

It was during this spell that he told his wife, before a trip, that he would not return. He engaged one of the latest U-boats, equipped with anti-aircraft guns, and though one of his depth charges destroyed the U-boat, one of her last shells hit one of the Liberator's engines, setting it on fire. The fire spread, the plane crashed into the sea and though the crew managed to scramble into their dinghy, Nelms was unable to break free. They spent 60 hours in that freezing inhospitable region before being rescued. Nelms' premonition had come true.

Lion At Large

Premonitions may come to one at any time and in any place and on occasions have been so urgent and pressing that those who have had them, have acted spontaneously and without thinking. This happened to Mr. H. Bernard of Brighton, who relates that 'while travelling with Bostock's Menagerie I left my wife and young son asleep in the caravan and went for an all-night card game in another caravan.

'At about five in the morning while in the middle of a hand I had a vivid mental vision of my son being attacked by a lion. To the amazement of the other players I threw down my cards and without a word of explanation rushed out.

'Passing the menagerie I heard a growl which told my trained ears that a lion was loose. Dashing inside I was horrified to see in the square formed by the cages, my small son sitting on the grass – and an escaped lion just crouching for a spring.

'In a flash I seized the loaded elephant gun that always hung at the menagerie entrance and taking swift but sure aim, brought the beast down in mid air. Its dead body fell on my son, breaking one of his legs.

'Had I stopped to analyse my premonition of danger or to explain to the others of that card party, my son certainly would have been killed. Since then I have never been able to fathom that sudden vision . . . it has always seemed to me like the supernatural and beyond man's understanding.

Mistaken Identity

Mrs. Florence Ellam, of Lewisham, then far more rural than it is today, said that in November 1934: 'My husband, a doctor, was awakened just after midnight by a loud ringing of the night bell. A farmer living two miles away had called him to attend his wife who was suddenly taken ill. My husband decided to walk there.

'I had a sense of impending danger and insisted on accompanying him but at the end of the drive he prevailed on me to return and set off by himself in the middle of the road. Half a mile from the farm he found himself confronted by three men who clearly meant mischief.

'The doctor, of powerful physique and an expert boxer, knocked out two of them and the third disappeard. Returning in due course to the surgery he found two patients awaiting him for treatment – one for a broken collar bone and the other for a fractured jaw! They had mistaken my husband in the dark for someone against whom they had a grudge!'

Only rarely are premonitions sound guides and unless they are overwhelmingly powerful it would be foolish to act on them. I know a women who gets into a fret the moment her husband sits behind the wheel of his car for she "knows" he is going to have an accident. She is such a bag of nerves that her "feeling" always brings on an attack of diarrhoea. Sometimes she becomes so upset that she takes to her bed. She is a trial to her husband, who is forced to travel a good deal by car on business. Her illness is psychosomatic* and is the result of her mental state. The

*From *psyche*, soul and *somatic*, body: the correlation of psychological phenomena, normal, abnormal, or pathological, with somatic or bodily conditions and variations.

mind is man's most powerful agent; if used properly it can bring health and happiness; if misused it can cause illness and even death. Unfortunately there is no differentiating between premonitions that bring warnings and the vague fears from which so many women suffer.

There are some, of course, who "feel" that ill luck or disaster is about to overtake a person they love, and this comes to pass.

The Hunch That Led To Fame and Fortune

One such hunch concerned Bette Davis the famous film actress, and changed her life. At the start of her career she had acted in a number of plays but always in parts of no importance. Then one day Frank Conroy gave her an introduction to George Cukor, who was producing "Broadway" at the Lyceum in Rochester, NY. As the smallest part in the show had not yet been cast Cukor, as a favour to Conroy, told her she could have it. It was only for a week but she left the theatre riding on air.

Her mother came to see her off to Rochester and just before the train pulled out, urged: 'Learn the part of Pearl. The actress playing the part is going to have an accident.'

As her mother was always having hunches, most of which came to pass, she laughingly agreed: 'Oh, mother! You and your hunches!' But she knew they were not to be sneezed at and even while on the train set about learning the part.

On the third day, during the Wednesday matinee, Rose Larner, playing the part of Pearl, slipped down a stairway and badly twisted her ankle. That night she managed to limp about with the help of a stick but her ankle swelled so badly during the evening that she was unable to carry on.

Bette Davis's reaction was not sympathy but elation, for she knew Rose Larner's part by heart.

Next morning she made it a point to get to the theatre early, but George Cukor was earlier. 'Get that dame who has the smallest part,' he yelled to the stage manager; 'fetch her right away.' He didn't even know Bette Davis' name.

'Here I am, Mr. Cukor,' she piped in her smallest voice.

'Can you learn the part for this evening?' he barked.

'I know it already,' came her answer.

'Come up here. Do you know how to fall down a flight of stairs?' Not for nothing had she trained under Martha Graham, who taught her all the physical tricks.

She nodded but Cukor was not convinced. 'Show me!' and she did. She went on that night to play Pearl, was a tremendous success and by the time the show had run its appointed time had planted her feet on the ladder to success.

Churchill's Sixth Sense Saved Him

Many famous men have been impelled to embark on certain courses by a sixth sense when logic has directed otherwise. Winston Churchill was one. He was a newspaper correspondent during the South African War and was taken prisoner by the Boers, but managed to escape and make his way by night through enemy territory and towards the British lines.

Eventually he came upon a small community and, desperate for food and water, decided to knock on a door and ask for succour. The community was a hostile one and it was some time before he could make up his mind which house to approach. Then his sixth sense came to his rescue, guided his footsteps and he knocked on a door. When it was opened he was relieved to find himself among friends. What was extraordinary is that it housed the only family in the district that was friendly to the British! Had he knocked on any other door he would have been handed over to the military and probably shot, a fate met by many who were captured, as the Boers regarded all Britons as spies.

Dr. A. L. Rowse

Dr. A. L. Rowse, historian and Fellow of All Souls, is Cornish and as a Celt, is prone to premonitions. He relates that while an undergraduate he was looking out on to the Meadows. The window was immensely heavy, of the sash type, and it suddenly entered his head that if one of the cords snapped and it fell on his head he would be seriously injured or even killed. He was in a despondent, resentful mood and said to himself: 'Let the damned thing fall!' Then suddenly he felt that it was about to fall and drew in his head – all in a second. The moment he pulled his head into the room the window crashed!

On another occasion when he was off-colour and thinking of nothing in particular he sauntered into the library and the thought came into his head that he would see two young assistants in each others arms. The moment he passed through the door he found them disengaging.

Rowse noticed that premonitions came to him only when he was off-colour, which seems to indicate that the mind and the physical body are inter-related, which bears out the James-Lange Theory, and he says in his book: 'It is less to be wondered at that the medieval and primitive people are so liable to the phenomenon of possession.'

On a third occasion Rowse spent the night of 18th June restlessly. It followed the week of Schools, which had taken a great deal out of him mentally and physically and he "knew" that something very unpleasant had happened to a member of his family. The moment he arrived home he learnt that his sister's child Reggie, the only one of her children known to him, had died in California on 18th June.

His father was also given to premonitions, for one night an old clock on the kitchen mantelpiece which had been "dumb" for years, suddenly started to strike the hour. 'That's an omen of death,' said the old man; 'I can feel it.' A few days later news arrived that his youngest brother had been killed in a mine accident in South Africa on the day and at the exact time the old clock had started to chime after its long silence.

David Niven's Wife

David Niven, the popular British film star, married his first wife, Primula Rolla, eights days after they met and she died not long after, in 1946, in an accident. Later he met the Swedish actress Hjordis and they married within ten days. Hjordis is a sensitive. She can "smell" bad health and knows when she is about to fall ill. She also knows when her husband is about to fall ill, and that well in advance. In addition, she has premonitions which come to pass.

'Once when we were in Rhode Island on a shoot,' said Niven; 'she refused on one occasion to come out with us, her reason being that she would be shot. We laughed and told her to be sure to wear a thick coat . . .

' "I'll come," she said; "only if you all insist."

'Well, we all insisted – and 20 minutes later she was shot. She got five pellets in her cheeks and seven in her neck and bosom. And there were 12 witnesses who had heard what she said earlier. How can you explain that?'

As already stated, a sixth sense can in some instances, be acquired by the use of drugs, though one would be ill advised to try this method. It happened, however, inadvertently and quite by chance, to the Hon. Mrs. M. Simpson (formerly Fitzpatrick), who stated: 'Under the terms of his late uncle, Lord Castletown, my husband inherited the old family home of Granston Manor, Co. Leix.

'We were married in January 1939. Six weeks later my husband, Col. Geoffrey H. J. Fitzpatrick, took me to Ireland to see my new home. We stayed with friends. Two days after we arrived my bridegroom was taken ill. I nursed him day and night and was relieved by two nurses. Assured that without a good night's rest I should collapse, I agreed with the doctor's suggestion to go to bed after an injection.

'As the drug began to act my sixth sense awoke. I saw the future. Too giddy to move, I rang for help. From the sick room below came the doctor and a newly arrived consultant. As in a dream I said: "Please arrange that the day nurse remains on duty until midnight tonight."

' "Why?" asked the doctor. "There's a night nurse."

'I replied: "Because my husband will die before midnight and I want both nurses to be there."

'I just remember the doctors looking at each other in astonishment as I fell asleep.

'My husband died that night at 11.30.'

When Should One Disregard a Premonition?

Premonitions are by no means a sure guide to the future and each individual has to decide when to obey the urge and when to ignore it. There is no hard and fast rule. In April 1972 Mrs. Margaret Woellner was preparing dinner in her home in Berlin when her ten-year-old son burst in. His eyes were popping and he seemed in the grip of unreasoning fear. 'Mummy,' he screamed in terror; 'get out of the kitchen quickly. At once! Something terrible is going to happen.'

The blood had drained from his face and he was so distraught that on impulse she grabbed her three-year old daughter Ulrike and all three bolted from the kitchen. They had scarcely covered more than a few yards of the garden than an explosion hurled them to the ground, fortunately without hurting them. Their home which had only recently been built, was completely demolished because someone had accidently ignited a leaky gas main.

When Mrs. Woellner asked her son for an explanation for his behaviour, he said: 'Really, I don't know. I just had this strange feeling that something terrible was going to happen. It was as if there was a voice saying: "Go and fetch your mother and sister, otherwise it will be too late."'*

Professor Hans Bender, head of the parapsychology department of the University of Freiburg, says: 'There are people who have a sixth sense. For years we have been investigating similar cases where people have known that something tragic was about to happen. Mostly such cases take the form of dreams and visions. In children this so-called sixth sense is often pronounced.' It certainly was in this instance.

He Knew His Time Was Running Out

Johnny Copley went to an elementary school and then took a job as a turner on a lathe. After a few years he and his brother Leslie each put down £15 and bought two cars from a scrap heap for £25. These they repaired and sold for £45 and £35 respectively. They then bought other cars and renovated them, making from £35–45 on each. In a year they had enough put by to buy a showroom and in two years were making £100 a week apiece. Their next move was to enter the car hiring business, which did so well that Johnny Copley owned a £6,000 Cadillac and the future seemed extremely rosy.

In 1957, however, he became moody and miserable. 'My time is running out,' he told his wife. I've been too lucky. I have a feeling I shall be killed.' How, he could not say. But he loved speed and felt he would die in a car accident. His premonition proved accurate for he was racing along Tower Bridge Road at more than twice the legal speed limit when his Cadillac went out of control and crashed into a wall. Five men and two girl passengers escaped unhurt but his body was impaled by the steering wheel and could not be dragged from the blaze.

Sunday Express: 2.4.1972

He Waved Good-Bye For The Last Time

Eddie Prior of Harans Cross, Swanage, Dorset, had six very good friends who belonged to his youth club. But when one morning in October they piled, laughing and joking, into a van to set out on holiday, he knew they were going to have an accident and would not come back. 'I can't see them coming back,' and he broke down and cried.

His final words to them were: 'Good-bye and take care,' which are the parting words of thousands of motorists every day; but this case was different. 'Suddenly in my mind,' he said; 'I could see they were not coming back. There was going to be an accident. I had a picture flashing in my mind of their van coming down a road into a motorway – and that was it! All over the weekend I had the same feeling. They weren't coming back.'

Although on their first stop they phoned to say that everything was going splendidly, Eddie was unhappy. Then, as they entered the A6 near Keele on their way to Blackpool, their van crashed. Three of them were killed and three badly injured. Why he had the premonition and not their parents, will never be known. Nor was Eddie, a labourer, a sensitive person, for William Mitchell, an official of the club, remarked: 'I know Eddie and no one can say he is the emotional type.'

Like those who live next to Nature, people constantly in danger, or who risk their lives, or whose job it is to deal with criminals, such as detectives, develop a sixth sense and are subject to premonitions and hunches.

When criminals produce perfect alibis, for instance, some detectives "feel" instinctively that there is something wrong with them, and by digging unearth the truth. This happens to frequently that the too-perfect alibi is usually queried. Spies belong to another group who keep alive because they have hunches which they obey; if they ignored them they would die or be captured.

Marguerite Smith, OBE

Marguerite Smith, part of whose story is told in the film "School For Danger," was awarded the OBE and the Croix-de-Guerre for services during the Second World War. She records many instances of hunches which saved her life and those of her colleagues from capture and torture.

She was reared in France, worked in the Renault factory and spoke the language more fluently than her mother tongue. In 1939 she returned to Britain and in September volunteered for the WAAF at Halton where, after training she was attached to Bomber Command HQ. Because of her intimate knowledge of France and the ways and customs of the people she was assigned to the organisation built up by Colonel Buckmaster, to operate with the Maquis behind the French lines. After a period at a parachute school in the north-west and at a firearms school outside London, she finished her training at the Security School where agents were taught what to do when dropped over France, and how to act if captured.

After a rigorous course of training she was ready for her first drop, accompanied by a man named Noel, a W/T operator. Both were to work with Jean-Marie, head of a resistance group in the Yonne area of Burgundy.

On reaching what they thought was to be the dropping area the hatch on the floor of the Liberator was opened and Marguerite sat with her legs dangling in mid air. They were travelling through cloud at the time and in the next second or two she would have been in the air. Then suddenly, Noel had a hunch. 'No, no!' he shouted: 'don't go!' She held back and as they emerged from cloud she could see a wide stretch of water glistening in the moonlight. Had she gone it would have been her first and only drop.

Hunch Found Valuable Documents

After some weeks in France news came through that a German agent had been killed by the Resistance and buried hurriedly in a lonely hillside, and with him some valuable papers; but as rain and wind had removed all traces no one could locate the grave.

Jean-Marie, Noel and Marguerite tried repeatedly to find the spot, but without success. Then she had a hunch. 'Give me a spade,' she cried, and hurried to a patch some distance away. There she started frenziedly to dig and after a few minutes her spade struck a body. 'Here it is,' she pointed and left the rest of the digging to the men, who unearthed the body and the papers.

Knew She Was Being Watched

On another occasion she stayed with an Italian family named Bassini and accompanied by Mme Bassini went into the village to buy a pair of shoes. After about three minutes she had a presentiment that she was being watched and told her friend. Most women would, in a panic, have quickened pace in an effort to escape, but her friend had a better idea. They walked straight into the Kommandant's office where they remained for half an hour, talking and joking and pretending to discuss the commandeering of milk supplies by the Army. When they emerged their follower had vanished for he thought that if they were accepted by the Kommandant they must have been genuine.

The Premonition That Came Too Late

The Resistance officer who had invited Marguerite to join the Corps was betrayed by a man named Roget, a double-agent. After a while she was overcome by a powerful premonition that Roget was on the side of the Germans, and warned Jean-Marie; but her warning came too late. Roget, working swiftly, told the Auxerre of his suspicions, and Jean-Marie was captured in August 1944 and sent to Buchenwald where he died.

Field-Marshal Lord Roberts, VC

Military commanders are not always the earthy, unimaginative types most people think they are. A successful general must imagine what his opponents will do, and try to counter their moves. Field-Marshal Lord Montgomery, the best British general thrown up in the Second World War says he had a strong feeling that he was destined to save his country in a coming war and after the death of his wife concentrated all his energies to mastering the arts of war.

Lord Roberts, another Celt, frequently had premonitions, which he invariably heeded. In his autobiography* he relates a number of examples. During an action in India an ensign in his

---

Forty One Years In India: Field-Marshal Lord Roberts, VC

regiment was killed and one of the enemy was making off with the standard when Roberts confronted him. The man drew his pistol and aimed it at Roberts who instantly "knew" he would not be hit. So spurring his horse forward as the man pulled the trigger he cut him down and rescued the flag. The pistol had misfired!

On more than one occasion either intuitions or premonitions forced him to over-rule military judgement. Once when in Afghanistan he wrote: 'My intention when I left Kabul was to ride as far as the Khyber Pass. But suddenly a presentiment made me retrace my steps and hurry back to Kabul – a presentiment of coming trouble which I can only characterize as instinctive.

'This feeling was justified when, about halfway between Buthak and Kabul I was met by Sir Donald Stewart and my Chief of Staff. They brought me the astounding news of the total defeat of Brigadier-General Burrows' brigade at Maiwand and of Lieut-General Primrose, with the remainder of his force, being besieged at Kandahar.'

Without delay Roberts set off for Kandahar and by a series of forced marches reached the capital and surprised the Afghans who had no idea that a relieving force was anywhere near; and because of this the Afghans were utterly defeated and the garrison saved.

Field-Marshal Foch

Field-Marshal Foch, a devout Catholic, also acted on hunches and premonitions. During the Battle of the Marne in 1914, he said: 'Reason and military precept were thrown to the winds as I followed an irresistible urge which drove me against all logic and reason. I advanced four miles. Why? I don't know. But I knew God was there and I was filled with a wild obstinacy.'

His experts advised him to turn back but he brushed aside their fears and warnings and though his position was extremely precarious, held on, and to the amazement of Joffre, his Commander-in-Chief, established his position and drove the Germans back. Later Joffre described it as a miracle but Foch's only comment was: 'It was given to me that I knew what steps to take.'

Field-Marshal Lord Kitchener

To all who came into contact with him Lord Kitchener seemed a dour, taciturn man. But his family had lived in Ireland for centuries and some of their "feyness" must have rubbed off on him. He was superstitious enough to consult Cheiro (Count Louis Hamon), the famous palmist about his future and even asked: 'How will I die? Will it be in battle?

'No,' answered Cheiro; 'you will die by water.'

On the strength of that Kitchener took lessons and became a powerful swimmer. Cheiro even told him the year in which he would be drowned and Kitchener often laughingly told his friends that he would end by drowning.

A few days before he was due to sail for Russia in 1916 he secretly visited Cheiro, who confirmed that the end was near.

As he was about to board 'HMS Hampshire,'' on his final voyage, he clasped the hand of Detective Inspector McLaughlan of Scotland Yard, who was his personal bodyguard, and said: 'Good-bye, my boy. God bless you. I shall never see you again.' McLaughlan was taken aback for Kitchener was the most undemonstrative of men.

Shortly after a gale blew up and the vessel either struck a mine off the Orkneys or was torpedoed – no one knows for certain – all on board except eleven lost their lives, Kitchener among them.

Some 30 years later I visited Countess Hamon at her home outside Chichester, where she told me the whole story. She and her husband were sitting before a blazing log fire on the evening of 5th June 1916 – the day and time the "Hampshire" went down, talking about Kitchener, when a large wooden shield with the Hamon coat-of-arms painted on it, fell with a crash from the hook supporting it.

'Kitchener,' remarked Cheiro; 'has been drowned. He knew it would happen like this.'

On inspection it was found that the hook had snapped.

SECOND SIGHT

Second sight is a term employed by Celts for prevision; for seeing an event before it has taken place, or a person who is elsewhere. Those who do not possess this gift think there is something odd about such people, or that they are imagining or making up the who thing. 'You know,' they say; 'how the Irish and the Welsh love to dramatise and exaggerate. They live in the world of make-believe.'

The Witch of En-Dor

One of the earliest examples of second sight concerns the Witch of En-dor who lived about the year 1056 BC. The Bible tells us that Saul said to his servants: 'Seek me a woman that hath a familiar spirit, that I may go to her, and inquire of her. And his servants said: "Behold, there is a woman that hath a familiar spirit at En-dor." '

So, Saul disguised himself and accompanied by two men, went to the Witch one night and asked: 'I pray thee, divine unto me by the familiar spirit, and bring him up, whom I shall name unto thee.' But the Witch had the second sight and instantly penetrated his disguise.

Though the Bible contains many examples of second sight and prophecy, and the Vatican Library houses the finest collection of ancient astrological books, the Christian Church has for centuries frowned on prophecy and reprimanded the laity when they professed a belief in second sight, for only the saints are expected to possess such powers.

Scientists have tried to explain second sight but have never succeeded satisfactorily. Dr. F. W. Edridge Green, oculist, examiner and adviser on vision to the Ministry of Transport in 1944, said: 'The most important thing to remember about vision is that if you are convinced you are going to see a thing, you will see it.' He quoted the Indian Rope Trick as an example. 'You see because you think you are going to see.' A suggested impression may appear so vividly before the mind that it overpowers the real impression.

'I was once travelling by train to Hampstead and firmly

believed that I had passed Belsize Park and that the next station was the one I wanted. When the train reached Belsize Park I looked out of the carriage window at the signboard and saw Hampstead there as I expected and got out of the train, but soon noticed that I had alighted at the wrong station.'

This is something that happens when you look at a page and read a word that you think should be there, but in fact, is not. It is merely a trick of the mind; an optical illusion, and has nothing to do with second sight, but scientists dislike accepting anything for which they cannot find reasons. They find it difficult to accept phenomena outside their limited range.

Possessors of second sight see visions they could not possibly have imagined and more often than not are most unlikely to have thought about.

The Brahan Seer

There are innumerable examples of people seeing things they could not possibly have imagined. Kenneth Odhar, Seer to the Lords of Seaforth and Mackenzie, who was murdered by the wife of Chief of the Clan on trumped up charges, foresaw their doom after being led to the barrel of blazing tar into which he was thrown. Before going to his death he clapped his famous "gazing stone" to his eye, which enabled him to see into the future, and began:

'I see into the future and I see the doom of my oppressor. The long descended line of Seaforths will, ere many generations have passed, end in execution and sorrow.' Then he began to retail the list of disasters which would befall the clan.

The Curse of The Seaforths

(1) 'I see,' said Odhar; 'a chief, the last of his house, both deaf and dumb;

(2) 'He will be the father of four sons, all of whom will follow him to the tomb;

(3) 'He will live careworn and die mourning, knowing that the honours of his line are extinguished forever, and that no future chief of the Mackenzies will bear rule at Brahan or Kintail;

Prophecies Of The Brahan Seer: Alexander MacKenzie, FSA (Scot) – Eneas Mackay 1924

(4) 'After lamenting the last of his sons he will sink into the grave;

(5) 'The remnant of his possessions shall be inherited by a white-hooded lassie from the East, and she is to kill her sister;

(6) 'And as a sign by which it may be known that these things are coming to pass, there shall be four great lords in the days of the deaf-and-dumb Seaforth – Gairloch, Chisholm, Grant and Ramsey – of whom one shall be buck-toothed, another hare-lipped, the third half-witted and the fourth a stammerer;

(7) 'Chiefs distinguished by these personal marks shall be allies and neighbours of the last Seaforth; and when he looks round and sees them, he may know that his sons are doomed to death, that his broad lands shall pass to the stranger, and that his race shall come to an end.'

At which he tossed his gazing stone into a nearby pool and calmly awaited his death.

Eminent Scots families who knew the Seaforths well, have noted that every detail of the vision was fulfilled when in 1860 the final prediction came to pass. Among those who attested to the accuracy of the Seer's vision was Sir Walter Scott, a friend of the last Seaforth; and Sir Humphrey Davy, the scientist.

The Brahan Seer's "crime" was to speak the truth when the Countess of Seaforth, a jealous female, summoned him and asked him to gaze into his stone. 'Where is my husband,' she demanded; 'and tell me what he is doing in Paris?' The Earl, a tall handsome man, had gone to France on business after the Restoration of Charles II.

Odhar turned to her and said: 'Be satisfied. Ask no questions. Your Lord is well and merry.'

The use of the word "merry" was unfortunate for the Countess had heard rumours that her husband was enamoured by a renowned French beauty, so she assembled her retainers and in front of them commanded him to tell her the full truth. Reluctantly he spoke: 'I see Lord Seaforth in a gay gilded room, on his knees before a beautiful lady, with an arm around her waist.'

This so enraged the Countess that she screamed: 'You have defamed a mighty chief in the halls of his ancestors, for which you shall die!'

He was publicly burnt alive on the Chanory Point on the Black Isle.

Odhar made a long list of prophecies, of which this was only one and the best known. One, which seemed most unlikely at the time, looks like coming true in the future. 'However unlikely it may appear now,' he said; 'the Island of Lewis will be laid completely waste by a destructive war.' Lewis, part of the Outer Hebrides off the west coast of Scotland, was an island hardly to be coveted by anyone in his senses; but just south of Lewis lies the island of South Uist, one of Britain's secret rocket testing sites. Should nuclear war break out, which seems possible in the not too distant future, both Uist and Lewis are likely to be obliterated, and another of his prophecies will have come to pass.

Sir Cedric Hardwicke

In 1914 Sir Cedric Hardwicke, then a comparatively unknown actor, toured South Africa in W. R. Paterson's Company. On 4th August the witch doctors said that they had seen a vision in the sky of a lion being attacked by a bull, which they interpreted to mean that England was being attacked by a powerful enemy. Everyone who heard it chuckled at such superstition and said it was preposterous. It happened, however, that the Germans had cut the telegraph cables on 4th August and there was no official news for four days, when the declaration of war by England came through. Then they all wondered how it was the witch doctors knew!★

Major-General Wilcox was in India at the time and in his autobiography published after the war, he said he was talking to a yogi a few days before war broke out, and the mystic said to him: 'I can see a lion being attacked by an eagle. There is a long and furious encounter in which both will be badly injured, but in the end the lion will triumph.'

'What does it mean?' asked Wilcox.

'I do not know exactly who will be the enemy, but Britain is going to be attacked very soon.'

Both Germany and Russia had eagles as their emblems but as Germany had close ties with England and the "Russian menace" had for years existed on the North-West Frontier of India, Wilcox assumed that there would be serious trouble on

★*A Victorian In Orbit:* Sir Cedric Hardwicke

the border. He warned the Commander-in-Chief; but a few days later German troops over-ran Belgium.

Field-Marshal Roberts, VC., Had Second Sight

Field-Marshal Roberts not only had premonitions but actually saw events before they occurred. On 29th July 1908 at the opening of the Plains of Abraham, Quebec, as a public park, he said: 'They refuse to believe me, and we sleep under a false security, for I do not hesitate to affirm that we shall have a frightful war in Europe, and that England and France will have the hardest experience of their existence. They will, in fact, see defeat very near, but the war will finally be won by the genius of a French general, named Ferdinand Foch, Professor at the Military School in Paris.' His speech was fully reported in the Quebec newspaper "L'Evenement."

Why did he name Foch, who was a Second Lieutenant in 1874 and by 1908 had been given no opportunity of handling troops in actions of any importance. And by 1914, having reached the prescribed military age for retirement, he was not retained in any command, though he was retained on the active list. He was utterly unknown in England.

On the evening of 29th July 1908 Roberts gave an interview at the Chateau Frontenac to W. L. Richardson, Editor of the "Winnipeg Tribune," George S. Robbins of "Chicago Daily News," Louis Marsh of "Toronto Star," Edward Corbeau of "L'Evenement," and four other newspapermen, to whom he repeated his prophecy.

'Let me add,' he told them, 'that England and France will have the most trying experience of their existence. They will, in fact, come so near to defeat that they will be fortunate to maintain their democratic status.'

'You do not envisage defeat with yourself as Commander-in-Chief?' his hearers asked.

'I shall not be in it at all,' answered Roberts. 'I've had my day, but as a prophet I make one more prediction. There is today in the Ecole Militaire in Paris a professor by the name of Foch who is destined for everlasting fame in military history. He is the man who will see us on the side of victory, what little victory there remains when it is all over.' They were eager to ask more question but as the Lieutenant-Governor was announced, the interview was ended.

The Prophecy About George Washington

In 1770, accompanied by his friend Dr. Craik, George Washington went on an expedition into the wilds of western Virginia. There he was visited by a party of Indians led by a grand sachem. The Chief approached Colonel Washington and said he knew him instantly although he had seen him only once, and that when opposed to him in battle. After salutations and expressions of goodwill had been exchanged, he said to Washington: 'On the day I first beheld you, I ordered my young men: "Mark yon tall and daring warrior. Quick, let your aim be certain and he dies." My warriors fired and killed many, but a power mightier far than we shielded you from harm. He cannot die in battle.

'I am old,' continued the Chief; 'and soon shall be gathered to the great council fire of my fathers, but ere I go there is something bids me speak, in the voice of prophecy. Listen! The Great Spirit protects and guides your destiny. You will become the Chief of Nations and a people yet unborn will brand you as the founder of a mighty empire.'

The Chief's prophecy came true in detail. Washington became noted for his reckless bravery and disregard for personal safety. Not once was he injured. An Indian warrior once fired at him from a distance of 15 feet – and missed! A cannon ball bounced between his horse's legs and richochetted harmlessly. He alone of General Braddock's aides survived the Monongahela massacre, and during the Revolution though exposed repeatedly to rifle fire, he emerged without a scratch. He was spared, as the Chief prophesied, to become the founder of modern America.

Second sight is far more common among the peoples of Africa and Asia, and aboriginal tribes, than it is in Europe.

The Arab In Aden

Emil Will Smith of Harwich, Essex, was a cable operator in Aden when he was 21. One day he met an Arab who said he could see into the future, so Smith challenged: 'Tell me what lies ahead.'

'Your life,' said the Arab; 'lies under the influence of Kismet. You will have much happiness but much sorrow in matters relating to your heart. Three times I see you at the altar, after you have been bathed in tears at the loss of two women who loved you as dearly as you loved them.'

'I married,' said Smith; 'four years later and I was a widower seven years afterwards. I married again in 1919 and again I was a widower in 1925. In 1926 I married for the third time. Everything turned out as Oman prophesied, for all my marriages have been blessed with great happiness.'*

In The Shadow Of The Pyramids

The uncanny way in which those in the East can "see" the future was described by Mr. E. G. Law of Kenton, Harrow. 'While in camp near Cairo,' he said: 'one day in 1916 I visited the Pyramids and ventured into one called Rameses II. When right inside my guide offered to tell my fortune, and so, seated in the stone case which had contained the mummy of Rameses, I allowed him to proceed.

'He told me I was an only son, with which I disagreed, as I had a brother. He said that on returning to camp I should find an important letter telling me of a death; that I should be going to England and afterwards to France.

'I should see many battles but would remain unharmed. Finally, I should meet a tall fair girl and a short dark one. The fair girl would try to make trouble between the dark girl and myself but would fail. The dark girl would one day become my wife.

'Being a confirmed bachelor I scoffed at this, but every word came true. I did receive that letter; my only brother was killed. I myself came through the battles of Ypres, the Somme, etc., unscathed. I duly met the two girls and there was trouble, but the dark one is now my wife.'*

There was no reading of palms, astrological charts or cards. The Egyptian just "saw."

The Arab Warned Him

Mr. M Hoyle, formerly of the East African Bureau, who retired to Birkby, Huddersfield, was also given an experience of second

*Sunday Dispatch: 6.10.1935

sight when one night in October 1917, on the eve of his departure from Lindi, East Africa, for a remote post in the interior, he was chatting with an Arab interpreter.

'He asked me,' relates Mr. Hoyle; 'if I believed that the future could be seen. I said "No."

'He then said gravely: "Then listen and take note. Your party leaves at dawn. The season is propitious, yet disaster awaits it. Even the water holes will fail you. *Not half the force* will reach its objective."

'I laughed for I knew the expedition was well timed.

'Next morning we started and our troubles began. An epidemic of strange diseases swept through the natives. We found the first water hole bone dry, and after intense suffering through thirst we lost half our supplies in the torrents made by a premature and unexpected downpour. We numbered three whites and 110 Africans on reaching the post against seven whites and 250 Africans on starting.'*

The Second Sight Of The Lapps

Lapland is heavily forested without tracks or paths through the trees, yet the Lapps seems to have no difficulty in finding their way through those trackless zones although the range of vision is seldom more than a few hundred yards. They have no maps or compasses; so, how do they find their way about?

Alexis Kivi paints a vivid picture of their methods and explains that they can pin-point any village or homestead for which they are making. Nor do they rely on the sun for in winter there is no sun, or so little and for periods so short that it might as well not exist.

He describes the way in which an old hunter living more than a century ago found his way about. 'No place existed, however distant,' he wrote; 'the direction of which he did not know without the error of a hair's breath, after a single visit. He pointed towards it immediately with his thumb; and it was in vain to argue with him, so firmly he trusted his own knowledge. If for instance, you asked him: 'Where is Vuokatti Fell?' he would answer at once, butting his thumb at the horizon: 'There, look along my thumb, over there. Couldst shoot it. Kuusmo

*Sunday Dispatch: 6.10.1935

Church is where that little dip is; but a tiny cock's stride to the right runs the line to Vuokatti Fell.'

A Lapp will set out to meet a friend 50 miles away in a particular glade, or beside a stream, or under a certain tree in two or three days' time, and he will be there at almost the precise hour; and without telling her, his wife will know to the minute when he is due back and have a meal ready.

If a friend 50 or 100 miles away wants help or wishes to do some business with him, his friend will know that he is coming and be prepared to meet and feed him.

A solitary life and contact with the earth and trees and water develops not only a sixth sense but second sight; life in a congested concrete environment kills it. Some years ago Robert Crockett, friend of, and an authority on, the Scolt-Lapps, said that when the Finnish Government decided to build a new village near Lake Inari, a deputation without being told about it, arrived. 'We have heard,' they protested to the authorities; 'that the huts are to be built only two kilometres apart. Will you use your power to have them built at least three kilometres apart for no one likes to live on his neighbour's doorstep and know everything that goes on inside his house.' They just didn't like living on top of each other!

Australian Aborigines

Till comparatively recently most Australians regarded the Aborigines with contempt and considered them to be so sub-human that in the remote Outback they used to ride out on Sunday afternoons and shoot them for sport, as they did kangaroos!* But anthropologists have convinced us that they are as intelligent as the rest of the human race and in some respects far superior. They possess a sixth sense that baffles the white man and they can "see" what is taking place a thousand miles away. Often they know when crimes have been committed in far distant places and communicate this information to each other over vast distances. The police have long recognised this and made good use of their powers.

They have a high moral and ethical code which puts the behaviour of white men to shame, and a religion which in many respects resembles Christianity; with a ritual like Holy

*The Black Man's Burden: Sydney Morrell – Sunday Express 3.6.1934

Communion in which the drinking of the blood of initiates and the "eating" of their bodies is undertaken.

The fact that they roam naked is not evidence of their backwardness but of their commonsense and it was the narrow-mindedness of missionaries that forced them to don ugly calico garments. Because they wander in an empty wilderness they are closer to Nature than almost any race in the world.

Seen 325 Miles Away

Some years ago a prospector named Laurie who owned a mine at Tanami in the Northern Territory, was asked by some Aborigines if they could drink from a water hole near his tent. He allowed them to do so but when they refused to move by dusk he ordered them to go and threatened to shoot them unless they did so. While he was threatening, a Warramulla woman who knew the leader, clubbed Laurie from behind. The Aborigines then fell on him but he fought his way clear, grabbed his rifle and wounded one of them in the shoulder, at which they fled.

The attack took place at eight in the evening. Two hours later two Aborigines who had been camping at Newcastle Waters 325 miles away, walked into the local police station and told the Inspector that a white man had been attacked and wounded by men of the Warramulla tribe and that they were helped by a woman whom they identified by her tribal name.

On being questioned they said they had "seen" the entire incident! There was no telephonic link between the two places and Laurie did not have a radio set. Smoke signals were out of the question for large tracts were completely uninhabited. The message may have been conveyed telepathically because every Aboriginal in the Newcastle area knew all about it as soon as it had taken place; but the two men insisted: 'I know 'im. I see 'im.'

The line of demarcation between telepathy and second sight in this instance, must have been tenuous indeed.

Kristen Zambucka

The New Zealand-born artist Kristen Zambucka, who travelled the South Pacific studying the Maoris, Polynesians and the

Aborigines is firmly convinced that the Aborigines possess second sight and are telepathic. She relates the story of Smoky Williams, of the Warrabi tribe who, while travelling in the guard's van of a train heading south for Adelaide, suddenly crumpled up with severe pain in his abdomen. Vivian Oldfield, manager of Amarroo Cattle Station who was also in the van, thought the old man was "putting it on.' Then Smokey straightened up and said: 'Pain gone. Daughter bin habbin' dat baby boy now.' When they returned home Dr. Mick Sturrell, who had attended the confinement, confirmed on questioning that Smokey's daughter had given birth at precisely the hour at which he had been stricken by pain.

Oldfield, a hard-bitten station manager, said: 'Talk about a missing persons bureau; they will give you the exact location if a missing person is 100, or even 1,000, miles away. I can ask my stockman: 'What's going on at Ooratipra?' and he'll reply: 'Them bin mustering now, Boss;' and they'll say who is working there and exactly how many cattle have been cut out of the herd. I've checked on it many times and they've never been wrong.'

An Aborigine in another part of Australia, when asked to explain his knowledge of an event which took place hundreds of miles away, replied: 'I just had a feeling. I not think of anything; then it come. I see. All truth is in dream-time;' or as we would put it, second sight. The *we-an* or witch doctor of the tribe is an adept at dream-time and can see events with amazing accuracy.

We send messages by radio and transmit pictures by television; we think we are superior because we have mastered certain physical laws but some tribes in remote parts appear to have portions of their brain so developed, or sensitive, that they can see and hear distant events without the aid of complicated apparatus.

The Strange Experience of Royal Davis

Royal Davis of Altadena, California, a chemist recounts a strange experience while on an expedition in Peru at an altitude of 14,000 feet. 'One afternoon,' he says; 'the mining engineer handed me a bag of ore samples and told me that it was imperative that Sample No. 20 be tested first, as he was going away and wanted a report by the following afternoon.

Davis' assistant, a Cholo Indian, had gone home a mile

across the *mesa,* so he intended leaving a note in the laboratory asking him to start on the test first thing in the morning; but as he had so much else to do, forgot. Early next morning he rowed out on Lake Pun Run to shoot duck and when about three miles out suddenly remembered the samples and, turning back, rowed in the teeth of a strong wind, arriving utterly exhausted.

He reached the laboratory at about four, to be met by Pedro, to whom he said: 'I want some samples tested, pronto.'

'She feenish, senor,' replied Pedro with a smile,' handing him the result, showing that Sample No. 20 had been tested first.

'But Pedro,' stammered Davis; 'how did you know that No. 20 was needed urgently?'

'Your *anima,*' explained the Indian; 'he coming in and telling me.'

'*Anima* means soul but with the Cholos it has a meaning all of its own. Their *animas* show them events that are taking place, or give them messages from distant places. When questioned for further information, however, they can give none and say: 'I see,' or 'I hear.'

Frank Ifield

Frank Ifield is a pop star who yodelled his way to the top of the charts with a song called "I Remember You." He is also an Australian with an affinity with the bush people. 'I remember,' he recalls; 'one of them was working in our show putting up tents when suddenly he said: 'I go home. My father he die.' Asked how he knew, he replied: 'I see him.'

As they knew the Aborigines, no one questioned the veracity of his statement, and sure enough, he returned to his people just in time to say a few words to the old man before he passed away.

Richard St. Barbe Baker

Wherever men plant trees the name of St. Barbe Baker, one of the pioneers of conservation, is respected if not revered. His efforts to encourage men in America and the tropics to plant trees, which bind the earth and bring rain and so transform arid areas into fertile ones, has saved many lives. For years he laboured as a Forest Officer in the Highlands of Kenya, with scant government appreciation or recognition for the valuable work he was doing. Then he left the service and returned to England and many years later returned to Kenya on a visit.

'As I drove on,' he wrote; 'I met Katootero my old gun-bearer. He was the first of my friends to greet me as I drove up to the forest station to inquire for him. I had not told him of my visit but he was obviously expecting me just as if he was keeping an appointment made overnight or the week before. Yet I had not written or sent any word or set eyes on him since January 1923 and it was now 1953! He had altered little in weight or in manner. He had the same gentle trusting look with just a hint of a smile playing round his mouth.

'Muthunga was Miti wa Miti;' he repeated the words as we held each other's hands in greeting.

'Tell me,' I asked; 'how did you know I was coming?'

'I saw you,' he replied.

'Where?'

He turned to the north-west and looked into the far distance by a steep angle of elevation in the bowman's way of showing the distance of a quarry. I questioned him further as to the country and he repeated: 'I saw you coming in the sand.'*

They Saw H. F. Varian Coming Across Thousands of Miles

Lawrence Green, a South African well versed in, and sympathetic to, the African's ways, gives many instances of second sight possessed by them. He says that in 1907 H. F. Varian, after building the railway from Lobito Bay to the Congo, completed another railway in Rhodesia and returned to Britain. Then he was offered the choice of work in the Sudan, Peru, Argentine and Angola and plumped for the last.

Months after his arrival he set up camp on the Cubal River, far inland, and one morning two weak and ragged Kaffirs approached and greeted him in "kitchen Kaffir," which he had last used in Rhodesia more than a thousand miles away.

'Don't you know me?' one asked in surprise, and then explained that his name was Antonio and he had been Varian's personal servant in Rhodesia. His companion was Varian's

*Dance Of The Trees: Richard St. Barbe Baker

former kitchen boy. The pair had trudged across Africa to meet him, starting from the Lower Zambesi when he left for London – long before he had been offered the job in Angola.

Repeatedly he questioned Antonio. 'How did you know that I would be there?'

'Each time came the reply: 'My heart told me so.'*

There isn't any logical or scientific explanation except to say that it must have been second sight that guided their footsteps.

Dom Moraes, the Indian Poet

Dom Moraes, the Indian Poet, who won the Hawthornden Prize at Oxford, once met a sorceress who possessed the gift of second sight. As his father was a famous editor of Anglo-Portuguese descent, he lived and was reared in the European tradition and had few intimate dealings with Indians. His father, however, knew that such people as seers existed and made an appointment for him to visit such a woman.

He was ushered into her presence and warned: 'Don't ask any questions. She will tell you what she sees.'

In the dim light of her sanctum he could see a puffy swollen face streaked with ash as is the custom with such people. Without a word being spoken by either Dom or his father, she poured out a torrent in Marathi, which a disciple translated.

Then she turned to Dom and spoke. 'You will travel across the black water (seas) and all your life will be spent in travel. In three years you will be famous and will do what you want to do. But,' she added with a finality that would brook no contradiction; 'you will never live in India.'

Within three years he had won Oxford's most coveted prize for poetry, which made him famous wherever English is spoken and he was launched on a career which enables him to follow the profession he loves. He is independent, has travelled widely on various assignments but lives in London with his English wife. It seems therefore, that the sorceress "saw" with considerable accuracy.

The Colonel's Orderly

While in command of a battalion of the King's African Rifles

*The White Man's Grave: Lawrence Green

85

Lt-Col. R. H. J. Ennis-Bruce had so many examples of second sight that he was not entirely surprised when one morning while going about his chores, Kwapativa his orderly paused in his work and remarked: 'The GOC is coming to pay us a visit, sir.'

'Really,' said Ennis-Bruce; 'how do you know?'

'I know' said the man, shrugging his shoulders. 'I see him.'

'When did he leave base?'

'Just this minute, sir.'

In spite of his knowledge about the powers of Africans the Colonel was not convinced. He got into touch with base by radio and asked: 'Is the General coming to visit us; and has he just set out?'

'Yes,' they confirmed the rumour; 'he left a few minutes ago. But how did you know?'

'Kwapativa,' was the Colonel's laconic reply.

'Oh, him again,' said his informant. At base they knew all about Kwapativa and his mysterious power.*

Commander Attilo Gatti

In Africa the second sight of the natives is usually explained as "bush telegraph" by white men, and though this means of spreading news over vast distances with incredible rapidity is normal, there are many instances of knowledge about far distant happenings which cannot be explained. Information is conveyed over deserts and immense tracts of water where drums and smoke signals would be ineffective.

Commander Attilo Gatti the famous explorer, wrote about an incident which took place in Mogadishu in 1924 when he heard his orderly exchanging views with another Askari, who said: 'The great king of the Engrisch has made a big present to our king.'

When Gatti asked what the present was he was told: 'The Engrisch king has given Italy a piece of land west of the Juba River.'

That evening when dining with the Chief Secretary to the Governor, he related the conversation and everyone laughed heartily. 'What nonsense!' guffawed the Chief Secretary.

Twenty days later, however, official confirmation arrived and subsequent documents proved that the gift of territory had been

*Star: 29.6.1951

made on the day Gatti's orderly had been given the news by his Askari friend. Nothing except second sight could have conveyed the news over thousands of miles of land and sea.

John of Howrah

More than 50 years ago there lived an old Hindu philosopher who, because he lived on the right bank of the Hooghly, opposite Calcutta, was known as John over the Water, or John of Howrah. Europeans consulted him surreptitiously for he was renowned for his gift of second sight.

A friend, Richard Ryan, who worked for a rice company in North India, had mislaid some documents which, if not produced by a certain date would lose him a large sum of money. Naturally, he was a worried man and as the day approached he ransacked his house but could not lay his hands on them.

As a last resort someone suggested a visit to John of Howrah and though at first he ridiculed the idea he realized it was his only hope. So he and five friends sought an interview with the mystic. After exchanging the usual courtesies John fixed his gaze on Ryan and announced: 'Six visit me but your problem concerns only one. It is not about death or illness or loss of money that you have some to see me; it has nothing to do with marriage or divorce or even a business transaction. It concerns the loss of important documents.'

He was lost in a reverie for what seemed an interminable period, then advised: 'Return home. Do not worry about your loss. You will lay your hands on the papers when you require them. Go! Believe me.'

None of the group had uttered a word about the problem. John had singled out none. There was no mention of payment, though they left some for charity.

Ryan was sceptical but did not resume the search. The night before the documents were to be produced, however, he found them under a sheaf of papers through which he had shuffled a number of times!

I have mentioned in one of my books* how John saw the disintegration and loss of the fortunes of my nephews, the

*Seeing Into The Future: Harvey Day

Sandalls, whose respected father, a lawyer, had left each one. On his retirement he entered the Church, probably in atonement.

Knowing from experience that lawyers in general are vultures who legally prey on the public, he urged them on no account to go to law; advice they disregarded entirely. What is worse, all except one were trained in the law.

When he died my Aunt Molly and each of her sons were amply provided for. They lived in a mansion on Ripon Street and their land was enclosed by Sandall Street, named in honour of the old man. The drive was so long that I used to gallop a pony down it.

Instead of being content to live on the interest from their capital and follow their professions they broke the bonds their strict upbringing had imposed. Their ambition was to travel and to see England but before setting out they decided to consult John of Howrah, who told them that they would fritter away their patrimony on drink, gambling and litigation. 'One of you will visit England,' he pointed at Tommy; 'but not as a visitor.' He was right.

Never has a family accelerated so swiftly to the dogs. The brake was off and the discipline of years thrown to the winds. They gambled on horses; they drank to excess; they speculated like men demented. They did everything to make their pious father spin in his grave like a gyroscope. Worst of all, they went to law on the slightest provocation for they thought they knew all about it. Their legal adviser, a Mr. Jones, told them not to; but they ignored him.

They borrowed from their dear old mother when their money ran out and when she was as featherless as a plucked turkey at Christmas they turned to the only member who had anything left – their brother Buddha, so nicknamed because he was supposed to be mad! He used to go to the local mosque and discuss theological issues with the *maulvis* (priests). They skinned Buddha as well.

Only one, Norman who became an architect, made anything of his life. The others were forced to take jobs as poorly paid teachers and tutors. As for Tommy – he saw England as predicted; but as a sergeant in the army during the 1914 war.

Experiences such as this tend to make one believe that the future has already been mapped out; that distant time exists and can sometimes be seen, and that we are but puppets on a world stage. Otherwise, how can one explain such happenings? My cousins were intellectuals, not idiots; they had been warned; yet they raced like lemmings to their doom.

The African Who "SAW"

Another example of an African who had second sight was given by a former Company Quarter-Master serving in India with the King's African Rifles. 'I was approached one morning,' he recalled: 'by my African storeman who told me he wanted leave. His reason was that his *shomba* (farm) in Africa had been burnt; he had lost four sons and his wife had gone to live with another man.

'When I asked for proof he replied: 'I have seen it last night.' Naturally, his application was refused as would the application of any British soldier on such flimsy grounds; but five weeks later I received a letter from the District Commissioner telling me that his farm had been destroyed and his wife had left him! There is little doubt that many "uncivilized" Africans have powers that baffle Europeans.'*

Mrs. Harker, the Irish Seer

James Halliday, an Indian Civil Servant in the days of the Raj, says that Mrs. Harker his mother-in-law was gifted with "the sight." She was Irish and often came out with prophecies in the most unexpected places. She was also a gifted astrologer.

One evening Halliday and his wife gave a dinner at which the guests included Muhammed Ali Jinnah and Mrs. Sarojini Naidu. At the time Jinnah paddled in a political backwater with little hope of either position or power. During a break in the conversation Mrs. Harker looked across at Jinnah and straight past, as if not seeing him. 'You,' she prophesied; 'may look down and out now; but one day you will rule your own state.' There was dead silence till with embarrassment Halliday branched out on another topic.

At the time Jinnah was a nobody in his own party but within a decade the Indian sub-continent was divided and he became the

*Star: 21.7.1951

89

Father of the new state of Pakistan. When she uttered those words nothing seemed more unlikely.*

Gipsies Have Second Sight

Gipsies are a race apart. They have roamed for centuries, never settling down to become part of any community. They are famed for their second sight. Though they ask that their palms be crossed with silver before they "see," they may not even glance into the hand and it is certainly not by palmistry that they know what is to be.

What The Gipsy Told Me

During the war I served with the River Thames Formation of the London Fire Service and when off duty was one of their lecturers who roved from Staines to Benfleet, Holehaven and Southend on the north side and Erith, Northfleet and Queenborough on the south.

One afternoon in January 1945 after giving a talk at Holehaven on Canvey Island, I entered the watchroom where one of the firemen said: 'We've got an old gipsy who often comes aboard for a chat. Would you like her to tell your fortune?

As I've always been interested in the occult this seemed too good a chance to miss, so I approached and asked somewhat sceptically if she would look into the future for me. 'Give me your hand,' she said; 'and without even glancing at it, intoned:

'You've been trying to leave your job and do something else. In two days you will leave and go to a place 100 miles from your home. You will live for about a year in a mansion which has been used as a hotel or something like that. You will be very happy.' She could see no more and could give no details. 'That is all I can see,' she said.

I did not believe a word. It seemed impossible. The doodle-bugs had ceased to fall on London and the V-bombs were so inaccurate that they gave the River Formation little to do. We were idling and wasting our time. For months the War Office had been trying to get me out of the RTF to lecture for them,

*A Special India: J. Halliday

90

without success. So the idea that I would leave in two days for a destination 100 miles distant seemed preposterous.

I cycled to Benfleet, took the train to Fenchurch Street and when I turned my key in the door of our flat in Chelsea my wife greeted me with the words: 'Mr. James has just phoned to say that Dr. Yeaxlee at Oxford has managed to get the War Office to release you. Will you phone Mr. James at once?'

I did so and was told to travel to Chadwick Manor, three miles from Knowle in Warwickshire, which is exactly 100 miles from London. Chadwick had been the home of a margarine millionaire named Morrison and after his death was run as a luxury roadhouse. During the war it was commandeered by the Army and became the HQ of the Midland section of the Army Education Corps. I worked there for 13 happy months, so that everything the gipsy saw came to pass.

I had two regrets only; that I was unable to get into touch with the gipsy and give her a gift, for my sanity had been saved. I was taken from a boring, repetitive job and given one that was creative. The other was in parting from five charming, stimulating characters who had been my colleagues.

Dr. Stockwood, Bishop of Southwark

I could tell scores of stories of gipsies seeing accurately into the future, but one more will suffice. Years ago when Dr. Mervyn Stockwood, later Bishop of Southwark, was a curate, he went on vacation and met a gipsy at a fete. As he was not wearing his "dog collar" she had no idea that he was connected with the Church.

She told him that he would return to Cambridge, the university from which he had graduated and that eventually he would sit in the House of Lords, near the throne. He did not believe a word!

Though most clergymen aspire to wearing gaiters, comparatively few imagine that a bishopric is within their grasp. Certainly Stockwood did not. But fate pushed him up the ladder and today he sits on the bishops' bench, which is near the throne. The odds against the gipsy making an inspired guess must be astronomical. She must have "seen" accurately.

Shane Leslie's Vision

Between the wars Sir Shane Leslie, the writer, was waiting at the Gare de Lyons waiting for the "Rapide" to take him to Marseilles when he remembered that his aunt, Mrs. Moreton Frewen, had seen a man murdered on the exact spot on which he was standing. As the thoughts flashed into his mind he saw the ghostly figure of a woman in black leaning against a pillar, muttering: 'He must change his train.' She continued to repeat the words.

The vision shook Sir Shane who knew instinctively that no one else had seen the woman for those around seemed to look right through her. He was certain that she was the mother of the murdered woman and the urgency of her tone and the way she looked at him indicated that the warning was meant for him. He was a Celt and believed in second sight, so acted instantly and told a porter not to put his luggage on the "Rapide" as he had decided to take a slower train which would reach Marseilles a day later.

On his arrival at Marseilles he was not in the least bit surprised to learn that the "Rapide" had crashed with heavy loss of life. Had he been on board he would undoubtedly have been a casualty.*

The Countess With Second Sight

Countess Elyce d'Armil, with whom I had a slight acquaintance, was an extraordinary woman. She was the seventh child of a seventh child and, as is well known, all such children have the gift of second sight and receive telepathic communications.

In 1915 when she was nursing the wounded in Paris there was near panic for rumour was that the Germans would soon be in the city. She was adamant that they would not and said to the Comtesse de Nouilles: 'The Germans will never reach Paris.' The Comtesse conveyed the news to Maréchal Foch, whom she knew well and Foch sent for her. He thought she had some secret information and asked: 'How do you know the Germans will not over-run Paris? How can you be sure? What is the source of your information?'

*Related by his son, Desmond Leslie

'I can "see," she explained. I have second sight.' And of course, the Germans did not take Paris.

After the war while travelling by liner to Montreal she went one evening to her stateroom for a bath and just as she had finished soaping she became aware of "an influence" nearby and heard a voice say: 'Fire - steerage - cabins 86 and 87.'

Without waiting to finish she slipped on her bath gown, found one of the Masters-at-Arms and gasped: 'Hurry - there's a fire in the steerage cabins 86 and 87.'

He did not ask how she knew but ran, and she followed. He broke into the cabins with an axe and smoke poured out. Two drunks who had fallen asleep while smoking, were inside. Their smouldering mattresses were quickly dumped overboard and the fire extinguished. The Master-at-Arms then thanked her and asked how she, a first-class passenger knew what was happening in the steerage as he had to make a report to the captain.

'I possess the gift of second sight,' she explained and made him promise not to mention her name as she did not want to be inundated by foolish questions and requests by inquisitive passengers.

Incidentally, she knew that Foch was the man who would lead the Allies to Victory and told not only the Maréchal but a great many others.

Voices Within

Voices often accompany second sight for those who "see" can also hear. Mr. Richard Poulton, a fishmonger of Peascod Street, Windsor, whom the Queen patronises, had a remarkable experience of this. Among his customers was Miss Frederica Hildrey, a close friend of his late wife. When she failed to call him for two or three days he found himself looking closely at his wife's photograph and heard a voice behind him say distinctly: 'Look after Miss Hildrey. Something is wrong with her.' At first he thought he was mistaken but the instruction was repeated. He decided he was having an hallucination but was so disturbed that he could not erase the incident from his mind, so went round to Miss Hildrey's house, knocked repeatedly, but could get no answer. He then called the police who broke in and discovered the old lady in bed with a heart attack. She was whisked off to hospital where she recovered.

The incident baffled Mr. Poulton, who could only explain it by saying: 'The link between the two women was strong enough to pass on to me.'

Premonitions and Second Sight

Irene Stewart's highland ancestry gave her the sensitivity to "see" and have premonitions, and both have come to her aid. What is more, she can turn her gifts on and off like water from a tap.

Her father volunteered for the Army in 1914 but was not sent to France till 1915. In 1918 when she was eleven she said to her mother: 'I shall have my daddy in my stocking (at home) for good and never hang it up again.' No indication had come from him that he was due for leave and she dreaded disappointing her daughter. Against her better judgement she allowed Irene to remain up on Christmas Eve till the last train from Lime Street, Manchester, had gone and then put her to bed with an 'I told you.' But the child was obstinate and persistd that her Daddy would be at home for Christmas.

They lived 20 miles from the city, cabs were few and motorists a rarity. Even so, at two in the morning her father arrived "on leave." When he got off the train motorist volunteers had met it and one of them had run him home.

Though he was only on leave, Irene insisted that he would not return to France. Nor did he, for the authorities discovered that he possessed technical qualifications which made him more valuable at home.

In 1939 Irene and her husband were living over a corner shop with their front door opening on to a side street, The Grove. From their bathroom window they could see right down the street.

One day she looked out of ther window and "saw" to her horror that the fronts of the buildings on the opposite side had been ripped away, making them look like battered dolls' houses, similar to pictures of homes destroyed by Nazi bombers during the Spanish Civil War. She could not see what had happened to the houses on her side of the street but assumed that something very big had fallen and sucked out their fronts as well. The vision persisted in her mind.

94

In May 1940 her husband was Senior Warden in the area and his youngest assistant was a girl under enlistment age, though none of them knew it at the time. For days she had been seedy but stubbornly refused to go sick. One morning Irene was hurrying across the street on her way to work when she saw the young warden and her mother on the opposite side with Death walking alongside the girl. 'Ah,' she thought; 'the poor girl is so ill that she will die,' and walked across to tell them that on no account was the girl to go on duty that night, so ill did she look.

That night a land mine fell on the girl's house, demolishing it and making an immense crater. The fronts of the houses on the other side were sucked out, just as she had seen in her vision. The ARP volunteers, whom she had told about her vision, were suitably impressed.

But that was not all. Three sectors of the ARP converged at a certain corner by a church, where wardens met after raids to ensure that none was missing. It was also a favourite rendezvous for a chat and a smoke, but shortly after the land mine had fallen in The Grove, she told the wardens: 'Stop congregating at this corner. It is dangerous.'

As they had ample evidence of her psychic powers her advice was taken, which was fortunate. She did not know why she said it, except that she had a premonition. Sure enough, a few days later, at an hour when normally they would have clustered there, the corner received a direct hit. The wardens were duly grateful. 'You can relax now,' she told them. 'There will be no more bombs.' Once again she proved to be a prophet.

Seers

Why do hard-headed businessmen and officials visit seers and clairvoyants? If asked whether they believe in such rubbish they would scoff. Yet many of them patronise such people because, lurking at the back of their minds most of them have a suspicion that the future can be seen. And in the midst of all the twaddle that most professional seers babble there is sometimes a grain of truth, like a pearl embedded in a mollusc.

Writers are supposed to be notoriously unstable people who let imagination run away with them. Philip Gribble records that on one occasion when he was in Ireland he was awakened by a voice which kept repeating: 'Buy Vocalions!' For three nights the advice was repeated, but he ignored it as Vocalions was a company of little repute whose shares stood at ten shillings. He wasn't going to be influenced by a mere voice. But it annoyed him when six months later he glanced at the *Financial Times* and saw Vocalions quoted at £17! Had he heeded the voice and risked even as little as £100 he would have made a packet. He decided that if ever he heard the "voice" again he would do as advised.

Fortunately he did, this time telling him to buy Corboda Central Railway shares. He was on to his broker like a shot and in a short time made a profit of 200%. Later the "voice" gave him the number of the winner in the frame at Aintree just before the Grand National; he placed a substantial bet, and cleaned up.

It was probably the Irish in him that enabled him to hear voices, for his mother had the gift of second sight. At the end of the Boer War she "saw" him in the conservatory of their home, dressed in khaki, with medals. 'You will do what Winston Churchill has done in South Africa,' she told him, but he put it down to a bit of blarney and a fond mother's wishful thinking.

After joining the army in the First World War, however, he transferred to the Royal Flying Corps and eventually replaced Liddell Hart as war correspondent on the *News Chronicle* in 1941. It took 40 years to happen – but it came about.*

Eleanor Glyn

All who have been transported into the world of romance by Eleanor Glyn's novels realize that she was a writer with a fertile imagination. She was also psychic and clairvoyant. David Herbert relates that between the wars she was a guest at a dinner party which included Prince George, later Duke of Kent. After dinner she was invited to see into the future, so went into a trance and prophesied: 'I can see the Prince of Wales's feathers dragging in the mud.' This infuriated Prince George, who refused to say another word to her for the remainder of her visit. Not long after she was vindicated by the abdication of the Prince, then Edward VIII.

On another occasion when she and David Herbert emerged from a cinema they spotted a poster, and a newspaper seller

Off The Cuff: Philip Gribble

shouting: 'Plane accident! Plane accident!' Air accidents were not as commonplace as they now are and Mrs. Glyn clutched his hand and said in a hushed voice: 'I can see the crash. You know four of the people killed on that plane and I know three.' And so it turned out to be for they were Lady Ednam, Mrs. Loefler, Sir John Ward and Lord Dufferin.

Towards the end of her life Eleanor Glyn lost her sight and when David Herbert and a friend, Michael Duff, visited her in 1943 she placed a hand on each of their heads and prophesied: 'I shall die within the next six months; but don't worry. The war will end in two years and neither of you will be harmed.' This proved to be accurate, too, for though both endured hardships and danger neither suffered a scratch.

What The Gipsy Told Lord Citrine

Lord Citrine, General Secretary of the TUC and the leading trade unionist of his time, had many experiences of the psychic. On one occasion while at Warwick with time to spare, he visited a fair where one of the booths advertised that a Madame X, 'patronised by the Lord Mayor of Liverpool,' Citrine's native city, was seeing into the future. He was intrigued and entered. As an appetiser she gave him a description of two colleagues with whom he was working in Manchester: one she described as 'a sticker' who would never move from his job; the other she "saw" was blond and wearing glasses. 'He passes things with his left hand,' she remarked, which made her assume he was left-handed. Both descriptions were accurate, the second applying to the General Secretary at the time, Jim Rowan.

Then she passed to prophecy. She told Citrine that his life was going to be transformed in the next two months for she could see him standing in front of several lines of windows. He would work there and it would be good for him.

Within weeks Citrine went for an interview for the job of Assistant Secretary of the TUC and as he turned into Eccleston Square, London, where the headquarters was, he says: 'I was struck by the array of windows, which stretched in even lines of four storeys right round the square,' and instantly recalled the clairvoyant's words. It was good for him for soon after he became General Secretary and a power in the land.

Citrine, of Norwegian descent, was also psychic with a strong affinity with the occult. He was attracted to seers like iron filings to a magnet and on one occasion was warned: 'Don't fly the Atlantic. Though nothing disastrous will happen, your flight will be extremely hazardous.' As he was a constant traveller, having been round the world three times, with trips to Australia and New Zealand, and 12 journeys to the States, he paid little heed to the warning.

It happened during the Second World War, and as he was walking down the slipway a voice kept repeating: 'Don't fly the Atlantic!' the advice that Kismet, the London clairvoyant had given him. But he had no choice.

On the return trip they called at Bermuda to take on heavy beaching gear, which kept the plane from flying at a safe height. They ran into violent storms; the plane was bombarded with hailstones, ice formed on the wings and they came down to within a few hundred feet of the sea. Then they ran into adverse winds. The plane was buffeted and none on board expected to survive. Instead of taking 24 hours the trip occupied 28 and eventually they touched down in Northern Ireland with only enough fuel for 30 minutes flying.

Lord Caradon

Lord Caradon, a Celt, is one celebrity who is not ashamed to confess that he visited a seer. After the Second World War he was transferred for six months from the Colonial Service to the Army where he helped in the fascinating task of establishing the administration of Cyrenaica. Then one morning he received a wire ordering him to travel to Jordan where his services were urgently needed. This infuriated him as he was in the middle of interesting, creative work. He went to Sir John Macpherson, his boss, to protest and then to Sir Harold MacMichael, the High Commissioner, but to no avail. Before going to Amman, however, he decided to visit Damascus, there to brood over the injustice of the world.

Late one night against his better judgement, he was persuaded to meet Victoria, a celebrated fortune teller. In a mixture of broken French and Arabic she told him not to worry and

*Two Careers: Lord Citrine

assured him that his future was extremely bright. 'I see,' she said; 'that within a month you will be transferred to a post much more to your liking.' As this seemed most unlikely he applied for ten days' leave to visit his wife and children who were in South Africa.

Before the month was out he flew to Cairo on the first leg of his journey to Amman and while at his hotel was called to the telephone. 'Don't go on to Amman,' he was told. 'You are to be transferred to Cyprus as Colonial Secretary.' It was there that Sir Hugh Foot (as he was then) used his knowledge and skill as a negotiator, to forge links between Greek and Turkish Cypriots and win the respect and confidence of both. It was there that he made the considerable reputation which led to his appointment as Britain's representative at the United Nations.*

Godfrey Winn's Mother

Another who entered a tent – this time a Unionist fete – to find what the future had in store, was Mrs. Winn, mother of Godfrey Winn, the well known journalist. She was then a bride of less than 12 months, so nervously she slipped off her wedding ring before entering the booth at Edgbaston. But the incumbent was not taken in when Mrs. Winn asked: 'What sort of a husband shall I have?'

'You have already chosen,' she replied; then after a pause; 'You will have two sons.'

'Your marriage will end in disaster,' she went on. 'There will be many black years ahead. But take heart; both your sons will end at the top of their professions.'

Everything that woman saw came to pass. Her husband, though a charming man, was an unregenerate alcoholic and her marriage a disaster. As "seen," however, Godfrey became Britain's most highly paid journalist; a man who wrung the hearts of millions of women each week by his sentimental articles, and when he died, left more than £350,000!

His brother Rodger, who was partly crippled, was a brilliant scholar. He became a barrister and ended as a judge of the Appeal Court.**

*A Start In Freedom: Sir Hugh Foot (Lord Caradon)
**The Infirm Glory: Godfrey Winn

Some possess the gift of second sight to a marked degree. To others it comes only in flashes. When Adrian Bell wrote a book about country life in East Anglia in the thirties no one thought it would sell as war reminiscences were all the rage. Books like Sassoon's *Memoirs Of An Infantry Officer,* and Remarque's *All Quiet On the Western Front* were selling by the hundred thousand. But on the advice of a friend he took it to Richard Cobden-Sanderson, who agreed to publish, adding: 'Don't expect to sell more than 500 copies as there is no interest in country life among the reading public.' How wrong he was!

When the book came out he was on a visit to his Aunt's home in Pimlico and arrived when her charwoman was reading the cards. Naturally, his cards had to be read, too. This perspicuent female held up the knave of spades and said: 'I see that your book will do much better than you think. It will sell in thousands!' At which they all laughed heartily.

But it did. So well in fact, that he was commissioned to write another in the same vein, *Silver Ley,* and after that *The Cherry Tree,* each of which enjoyed an astounding success not only in Britain but on the Continent and in America. They also became among the earliest and most famous of the Penguin Books.

Cards and crystal gazing come within the orbit of second sight.

Many film and stage people are fey. Most of them are extremely superstitious and practically all consult clairvoyants and soothsayers at some period of their lives. Van Johnson the well known film star, was no exception. He went to see Madame Ve-ara, whose consulting room in Oxford Street, London, is known to film producers, directors and actors, who constantly nip in to test her powers.

Van Johnson

When Van Johnson visited her she asked: 'Do you believe in this?' and his answer was: 'I do. I believe in everything. I even believe in Father Christmas.'

'Good,' she replied as she settled before her crystal ball. After peering into it for a considerable time she revealed: "You've been through a period of darkness but now everything will be all right. 1961 will be a wonderful year for you although you may not know it yet. I see a stage with young people on it, singing and dancing. And you are there. You are a great success.'

'I am?' he asked sceptically, for at the time his fortunes were at low ebb.

'You are,' she confirmed; 'but you are scared. Something about this stage scares you but there is no need to fear. It will be a wonderful year for you.'

Later Van Johnson confessed: 'That woman is wonderful. I opened in this musical "The Music Man" on 16th March and she tells me about it, including the fact that I'm worried about my breathing during some of the longer numbers; something no one else knows about.' It all came true as Madame Ve-ara had seen it. He was such a success in London that the Americans clamoured for him and it led to film contracts over there.

Vision

Visions are not confined to clairvoyants. Ordinary people sometimes have them, too. Mr. C. L. Seaman wrote: 'In the summer of 1933 I was in command of an oil tanker which was laid up at Queenborough Pier, Sheppey. My wife joined me on board.

'I was chatting on the sea front with another sea captain when suddenly I had a vision of my wife falling on the ship and being carried away. I hurried back to my ship where the Chief Officer told me that my wife had fallen through a hatch to the deck below – and was badly bruised.' What caused him to see her falling and why did the warning not come before the event?

The Royal Yacht

Frank Harrison, another connected with the sea and ships, also had a vision. 'Years ago,' he said: I had a good deal to do with the building of the royal yacht "Victoria and Albert" at Pembroke Dockyard. At the time about which I am writing she was in dry dock being prepared for her steam trials.

'On the day previous to her being undocked I was in the office near a partly open window when a passing dockyard engine clouded the window with steam. In the obscured window I saw a perfect vision of the yacht lying over on her side.

'That night I slept in the office in view of the early undocking,

· 101

and at about 5 a.m. a messenger reported that the vessel was turning over in the dock as the water was being shipped.

'When I reached the spot the "Victoria and Albert" was lying over on her side with her masts and funnels overlapping the roof of a dockside boiler shop, just as I had seen her in the steamed window.'

The Sight

Mary Nicholson also had the gift of second sight. 'The first time "second sight" burst upon me,' she wrote; 'it came not as a mental vision but as an actual picture visible to the naked eye, although its duration was for a few seconds only.'*

At the time she was engaged in the hum-drum task of washing the kitchen floor when suddenly 'as if thrown upon a screen' she "saw" her schoolboy brother who, with his father and a party of geologists, was exploring the countryside. The picture she saw was a section of mountainside from which a vertical slab had broken away, and directly below it was her brother. As it fell she saw the horrified face of her father, and then her brother, who had also seen it, swivelling to avoid it. It was all over in a couple of seconds but she knew that her brother had not been injured; nevertheless her vision was so real that it left her shaken and terrified.

She said nothing to her mother and the postcards which reached them from her father failed to mention the event. When they returned from their holiday, however, her father said: 'Did you know that Mike was nearly killed? It happened on . . .'

He was amazed when she broke in: 'On last Friday morning at ten minutes to seven.'

'How on earth did you know?' asked her astonished father. 'We didn't write about it.'

Then she explained how she knew and described what she had "seen".

Spirit Vision

"Spirit vision," commonly called second sight, is not so rare a phenomenon as some suppose. Many people have this faculty without knowing it.

*Prediction: May 1962

'We know in Paris a lady,' says Allan Kardec,* 'who possesses permanent second sight, and with whom it is as natural as normal vision. She sees without effort and without concentration, the character, the habits, and the antecedents of those who approach her; she describes disease and prescribes efficacious treatment with the greatest facility; it suffices to think of an absent person – she at once sees and describes him. On one occasion we were with her and we saw someone pass in the street who was connected with us but whom she had never seen. Without the preliminary of any question being put to her she very exactly depicted his moral character and gave us very sound advice about him.'

Madame Bardeau

Madame Bardeau who lived a hundred years ago possessed this singular faculty. 'She was able,' says Gabriel Delanne; 'to describe exactly people who lived far away in the southern provinces, and whom she had never seen, and was able to give details concerning their characters and circumstances. Nevertheless she was in a normal state, her eyes wide open, and she carried on conversation on other subjects, interrupting herself occasionally to add some trait concerning the face or character of the absent person which rendered the description more complete.'**

Long Sight

How far can a man with the most wonderful eyesight see? A mile or two; or if on a hill sixty or seventy miles. When I was at school in Mussoorie in the Himalayas, 7,500 feet above sea level, a wonderful panorama of the Indian plain spread out before us and we could see trains 50 miles away crawling like centipedes, and the smoke from them at a much greater distance. Some said they could see 200 miles on fine days! But for normal sight about

*Revue Spirite: June 1867

**Evidence For A Future Life: Gabriel Delanne

50 miles was the limit without the use of binoculars or telescopes.

In the eighteenth century Swedenborg, the Swedish philosopher, scientist and man of many parts, who often had visions, startled his companions by stating that Stockholm was on fire. 'Nonsense!' they retorted; 'how can you know. The city is 250 miles away.'

'I can see it,' he said; and then proceeded to give a detailed commentary on the progress of the fire, ending with the satisfying news that his house was safe.

Days later when the ews of the fire reached them his friends found that every detail of his description was corroborated. Was that an example of long sight or second sight?

Commander Gould

Lieutenant-Commander Gould, R.N. was an inveterate digger of unusual information and in one of his books gives the astonishing case of M. Bottineau who, after holding a minor post in the Navy of Louis XVI of France, was appointed Beacon-Keeper to the Isle of France, now Mauritius, in 1764. Two years earlier he had propounded the strange theory that when ships approached land they affected the atmosphere by sending out mysterious waves which trained observers could feel and in this way predict the arrival of vessels.

At first his colleagues scoffed but when he won a number of wagers predicting the arrival of ships 250 or more miles out at sea his remarkable ability was brought to the notice of the Minister of Marine in Paris.

In Mauritius on 15th May 1780 he foretold the approach of ships which reached the island on the 17th, 18th and 26th of the month, respectively. So convinced was Vicomte de Souillac, the Governor, that he offered Bottineau £400 a year with a pension of £50 a year for life if he would reveal his secret, but unfortunately he demanded more.

There is little doubt that he possessed some extraordinary power for between 1778 and 1782 he "saw" the arrival of no fewer than 575 ships, some of them four days' sailing distance away – and a few as far off as 600 miles from the island!

Eventually he returned to France, hoping to cash in on his powers but unluckily for him the Revolution burst on the country, and though he convinced Paul Jean Marat, France was in much too great a turmoil for interest to be aroused in Bottineau. It would have been well had he accepted the Vicomte's offer.

The Strange Case of Freidrich Kornat

The case of Freidrich Kornat, a German engineer, has long puzzled investigators into ESP. One night in 1926 while working in Brazil, he experienced a frightful vision in which he "saw" Jurgen, his eldest son, who had returned to Breslau to study at the University, being knocked down by a car, and the voice of a spectator saying: 'He is dead!' This so shocked him that he came down to breakfast white and shaken.

When he told his wife what he had "seen" she laughed at his fears. 'Oh, well, we all have nightmares! You must have eaten too much pie for supper.' She then phoned her doctor, who examined Kornat and said he had been over-working.

Next day, however, a telegram arrived which stated: 'Your son Jurgen died in a street accident.' The family returned to Germany at once and on checking details found that they agreed in every respect with his vision.

That was not his only experience of second sight. During the Second World War he "saw" his second son, Gunther, in a German hospital, dying of wounds and though for months no news of him had reached his parent, Kornat dashed to the hospital purely on the strength of his vision where he was just in time to spend a few minutes with Gunther before he died.

In 1952 he had another vision and wired his daughter Agnes, urging her to return home at once. She obeyed and they had a happy reunion. The next day her mother collapsed and died of a heart attack. He turned to his daughter: 'Now you know, Agnes, why I sent for you.'

His final vision occurred months later, causing him to leap from his bed shortly after midnight and rush to his office where he had "seen" burglars trying to force their way in, and was just in time to frustrate them.

Psychiatrists who investigated his case came to the conclusion that he had 'unusual telepathic sensitivity.' Which explains nothing.

105

The Vision of Miguel Fernandez

Miguel Fernandez, a poorly paid clerk who lived in Cordova, Spain, was not a gambling man for he had a wife and family to support and lacked the gambling instinct.

One afternoon while walking down the Calle del Conde Gondomar he was accosted by an Oriental who asked for a match.

This seemed but an excuse to hold a conversation and enlarge on the substantial prizes to be won in the National Lottery. 'Ha,' thought Fernandez; 'he wants to sell me a ticket.' He shook his head. 'I never gamble.'

'A pity,' said the man; 'because if I were you I'd make straight for Madrid and try your luck.' They parted civilly and Fernandez went home.

A few days later something prompted him to enter the Great Mosque. At first he saw nothing in the gloom but when his eyes grew accustomed to it he noticed the man who had accosted him a few days earlier, now dressed as an Arab. 'Go to the . . . office in Madrid;' urged the Arab; 'and buy a ticket.' Then he seemed to dissolve and vanish.

Who was the man? Had he suffered an hallucination? Was the fellow an ancestor? He made inquiries but could find no trace of an Arab in his family. Whereupon he took the man's advice, went to Madrid, bought a ticket and won 50,000 pesetas! He kept enough to give his family security and gave away the remainder for, being superstitious like most Spaniards, the thought of the supernatural sent a shiver down his spine.*

African Who "Saw" A White Man Killed

Many years ago Frederick Kaigh of Loughton, Essex, worked in Africa and experienced numerous examples of second sight and telepathy. 'At sunrise,' he says; 'one of my "boys" suddenly became very excited and told me that a great friend of mine had been killed by a charging elephant. As my friend was 90 miles away, I asked: "How do you know?"'

'I see it;' said the African.

'Then tell your friends,' said Kaigh; 'to make a stretcher and

*Answers: 3.7.1954

carry the dead man to a hotel-and-store near the spot where he was killed.'

Kaigh then drove a fast as he could to the place of the tragedy and when he got there the owner of the store said: 'Your friends' "boys" have brought him in on a stretcher. They told me you had given instructions for them to do so.' "Neither of us thought there was anything unusual about this," was Kaigh's reaction.

The Pigmies of Oubangi-Chari

Pigmies who live in the hinterland of Africa are among the most primitive people on earth. They are also highly developed psychics and extremely intelligent. They can "see" what is happening over vast distances, communicate telepathically, and think nothing of it. In July 1963 Herr E. M. Koerner told an unusual story which was printed in *Die andere Welt* (Freiburg im Breisgau) and *Heim und Welt,* a popular weekly, about a Frenchman, Jacques Mangeret, an agricultural expert who went out to advise a tribe of pigmies in Oubangi-Chari.

One morning a letter from home was brought to him by a pigmy maiden named Milla. On handling it to him she offered the information that it contained bad news. Though she knew not a word of French she had "seen" the death of Mangeret's fiancée's mother! The news made him fly to France without delay.

Milla, to whom he had been kind and was very much attached to him, seemed unconcerned at his departure. 'You will come back again,' she assured, but this seemed out of the question as he intended to marry and settle in France.

He did; but his marriage proved a failure and a few years later he was back with the pigmies to continue the work he had been doing.

He was astonished on his arrival in Oubangi-Chari to find the entire tribe waiting for him, and was entertained with drums, dancing and a splendid feast. 'We expected you to come today,' explained Milla when he asked how they knew. 'We saw you.' And, as is unusual in the case of Europeans, Mangeret was eventually married to Milla by the local witch doctor, and settled down to an idyllic existence in the jungle, unburdened by income tax, rates and fears of breathalyser tests.

The Vision and The Mamba

Sir Charles Ponsonby, Bart., tells of an incident at Port Herald, the southernmost town in Nyasaland, 25 miles up the line from Chindio, where an old-timer from India had retired. This Anglo-Indian was lolling one evening as was his habit, in a long cane chair with a glass of whisky on the ground beside him. He lived near the station and listened to the rumble of a train coming in. Then, as he was ruminating, he saw before him his old bearer from India, with a *kiboko* (small pliable switch) in his hand. Without uttering a word he flailed his *kiboko* down to the floor, smashing the glass of whisky.

The old-timer leapt to his feet indignantly, looked at the smashed glass and saw beside it a dead mamba, Africa's most deadly reptile, beside it. The Indian had vanished.

He ran to the station to find his bearer but no one had seen a man such as he described, either getting off the train or entering it. He inquired everywhere but there seemed no trace of the man.

Months later he received a letter from his old bearer asking him if all was well, and telling him of a dream that had disturbed him greatly. He then went on to describe the incident with the mamba, and was anxious to know whether his old master was well. The time of the dream and that of the incident were identical.*

Red Indian "Saw" Death 150 Miles Away

Jean W. Godsell firmly believes in second sight and the power of telepathy possessed by American Indians. In 1921 she spent months in the Canadian northland, cut off from civilization, for radios were not in every home and planes did not fly beyond the Dew Line at the time. One morning in the late fall she watched as the Caribou Eater Indians departed on their annual exodus east to Hill Island Lake Country. Among them were Marie and Therese Cheesie, daughters of the Chief, who were six and seven years old respectively. Both were laden with bales and bundles which weighed more than their tiny bodies and her heart went out to these tots as they slipped and staggered down

Ponsonby Remembers: Col. Sir Charles Ponsonby, Bart.

the steep bank. 'Poor mites,' she remarked to her husband, who replied; 'It's tough, but it's part of their lives.'

Then winter covered the land with her frigid blanket and months later when she was thawing out a loaf, their Indian interpreter, John James Daniels, burst into the kitchen. 'Injuns,' he said excitedly; 'dey come today.'

'How d'you know?' she asked. 'Not a soul has entered the fort for weeks.'

'Me know. Dey have plenty bad luck, too.' He pointed to the horizon. 'Dey come before the sun reach here.' He ventured no explanation for his prediction.

After lunch Constable Bob Baker of the CMP* dropped in and invited: 'Come for a hike to the river bank. You've been cooped up here for far too long. Some Indians are coming from the direction of Dog River. Let's see who they are.'

After a while they spotted on the ice, a dog team moving at caterpillar speed towards them, for there was no driver with a whip behind the sled to urge the dogs along. 'Look,' pointed the interpreter who was with them, and they spotted a tiny fur ball emerge from behind a hummock, ploughing a furrow in the deep rifts with snow shoes, and as the sled came into focus they saw another dwarf.

After what seemed an age five emaciated dogs, tugging and pulling, hauled the sled up the river bank in the wake of Marie Cheesie, while behind Therese flourished a caribou hide whip with shrill cries.

Daniels pumped questions at them, to which they gave monosyllabic replies; and when Mrs. Godsell asked: 'Where is their father?' he explained.

'Cheesie; him die way out in the bush eight sleeps to the east. Den kids – dey tie 'im on sled and trek 150 through de woods to bring 'im to de fort so mission people can bury 'im proper. I told you,' he added; dey come today.'

'But how did you know?' she persisted.

'Last night I had dream. I saw everything just as now.'

The dreams they have are not the sort that come to us during sleep. Their dreams can be induced at will.

Years ago at Fort Churchill the ration ship was so long overdue that the men were issued with gunpowder and bullets in order that they could supplement their dwindling rations

*Canadian Mounted Police

109

with caribou meat. Mr. Tremayne, the Inspector, was desperate. 'What on earth could have happened to the confounded ship?' he asked no one in particular.

'Why not ask old Shonkelli?' Ashton Alston, the Factor, crooked his thumb in the direction of the local medicine man who sat inscrutably puffing his pipe. The Indian knew, of course, what was going on in their minds and Alston knew that he would be induced to talk only if his "fee" was big enough, so they piled some tobacco on the counter. But he took no notice. Only when the pile assumed suitable proportions did he nod in agreement. Then bundling the tobacco into a leather bag he repaired to his wigwam, went into a trance and did not emerge till sundown.

'Me had'm dream,' he began as a preamble. 'I send my spirit body over water.'

They waited anxiously for the next instalment. ' "Nascopie" – she safe. She delayed to rescue marooned party from another ship lost in ice in Hudson Strait. But bad luck. One man wearing clothes like woman – he died and buried at sea. Tomorrow when sun in dere,' he pointed low in the sky to the east; 'white man's ship he come.'

Alston nodded. He knew his Indian; but Tremayne was sceptical. 'What a lot of rubbish!' he exclaimed indignantly. 'Impossible for him to see all that.'

Next morning, however, when the sun was low in the east, exactly as Shonkelli said it would be, a microscopic speck was spotted on the horizon, which quickly grew till the excited inhabitants of the Fort cheered with relief. Soon the familiar lines of the "Nascopie" were revealed.

Everything the Indian had "seen" happened. She had sighted the marooned crew of a foundered vessel on an ice floe, had gone to their aid and then had been trapped in an ice pack for days. And what about the man dressed like a woman who had been drowned?

He was a priest on his way to the Mission at Chesterfield who had fallen overboard, was drowned and buried at sea.

These are but two of the many authenticated cases of Indians "seeing" or "dreaming" of events that had not happened, or so far distant that news of them could not possibly have reached isolated settlements of white men.

Sometimes people who are not normally psychic have glimpses into the future. My wife, who lays no claim to having second sight has had two odd experiences. One morning she said: 'I had rather a frightening dream in which I saw a river overflowing its banks and a large bridge over it collapsing. There were people struggling in the water. It seemed so real. I think it happened in Austria, though why, I can't say.'

She dismissed it as one of those nightmarish deams one sometimes has and as there was no mention of it on the early radio bulletins, dismissed it from her mind. But when I opened *The Guardian* I saw on page three a picture of a bridge in Austria that had collapsed, with deaths by drowning of some dozens in the river below.

On another occasion she remarked: 'I read in my paper that a journalist has swum the Channel both ways. I thought you might be interested.' I was, for at the time I was writing an article on Channel Swimming, but after scanning my paper could find no report of the feat, so at lunch remarked: 'There's nothing in my paper about the Channel swim.'

'It was in mine,' she said; 'on page two, right at the bottom.' But a search failed to reveal it.

Next morning, however, the radio stated that Kevin Murphy, a journalist, had made a double crossing of the Channel, and the paper my wife reads first contained a report of the event at the foot of a column on page two just as she had seen it in her mind's eye 24 hours earlier.

Nicholas van Rensburg (1862–1925)

One of the most remarkable of modern seers was Nicholas van Rensburg, son of a poor Transvaal farmer, whose powers were so extraordinary that he was mentioned in the government Blue Book of South Africa in 1915.

He first demonstrated his powers at the age of ten when there was unrest among the Africans, who became so threatening during his father's temporary absence, that his mother decided to leave the farm for safety. But Nicholas assured her that she had nothing to fear. 'The Lord appeared to me in a vision,' he said: 'and promised to protect us.' This so impressed her that she stayed and almost at once the attitude of the servants changed.

He became renowned as a local seer, was ordained an Elder of the Dutch Reformed Church, married and worked on his own farm. After war broke out and the Boers had a succession of victories, he warned in the midst of jubilation: 'I have seen a terrible vision. Many farms will be burnt and men and women taken prisoner. This is no time for rejoicing.' No one believed him and his commander, who thought he was suffering from hallucinations, sent him home on sick leave, but in due course all he had seen came to pass.

His fame spread and the Boer leaders, among them General Hertzog, a future Prime Minister, consulted him.

An extract from Hertzog's diary bears witness to his high esteem of van Rensburg. 'He foretold a successful battle near Wolmaranstad and described how the enemy would move,' and gave details which proved accurate. He foretold how various engagements would go and the leaders came to rely on him and consult him before battle.

His most dramatic prophecy concerned General de la Rey, details of which appear in the Blue Book. He "saw" de la Rey's force in a precarious position and said he would extricate his force and achieve a notable victory. Which he did with incredible skill, capturing Field Marshal Lord Methuen and his entire force in the process.

After the war he told de la Ray of a strange dream in which he saw the number 15 on a dark cloud from which blood streamed. This was followed by the return home of the General, without a hat, followed by a carriage covered with flowers, which de la Rey interpreted as meaning high honour after a victory. So at the start of the First World War he planned a rebellion for 15th August 1914, which was postponed for a month, and on 15th September he joined rebel forces from other parts of the Union. By a coincidence, however, the police who were trying to capture a criminal that night, sealed off all roads leading out of Johannesburg and when de la Rey's car tried to leave the city, challenged it, and when the driver refused to stop, fired and killed de la Rey. Hours later he was taken home 'without a hat,' followed by 'a carriage laden with flowers.'

Smuts, though a scientist of considerable stature, did not let his training blind him to the value of Rensburg's powers and constantly consulted him. In 1924 when in political difficulty he sent for Rensburg, explained his problems and asked for advice. 'Tell me what you see. If it costs me my life I will follow your advice.'

Rensburg sat silent for a while, then shook himself and said:

'Dissolve Parliament; hold a General Election and you will be victorious.' Smuts did so, and was elected with an overwhemingly majority on 17th June 1924.

It is a pity that Rensburg did not live to "see" events after the Second World War or Smuts may have acted differently and the course of South Africa's disastrous slide into apartheid might have been checked, and a catastrophe which is inevitable, averted.

He "saw" during his lifetime, however, many events which came to pass, among them the Union of South Africa in 1910, the industrial disturbances in 1913 and 1914, and the influenza epidemic of 1918, which killed thousands. None of his prophecies proved wrong and none was so vague that it could not be identified when it came to pass.

TELEPATHY

Telepathy, a word derived from the Greek *tele*, afar; and *pathos*, feeling, is communicated by other than known physical means of thoughts, experiences, feelings, etc., from one mind to another across space, sometimes amounting to thousands of miles. Telepathy is now accepted by scientists as being possible as there are thousands of authenticated instances of such communication; and distance healing may even be a form of power projected by such means.

The Oracle At Delphi

One of the first recorded instances of telepathy occurred in 600 BC when King Croesus of Lydia, wishing to test the various oracles in his kingdom, dispatched several messengers to ask these oracles what the King was doing at an appointed hour on the hundredth day after their departure.

When that hour arrived the King took a tortoise and a lamb, cut them into pieces and boiled them together in a brazen cauldron fitted with a lid of brass, a most unusual activity for a king.

When the messenger dispatched to Delphi entered the temple, the priestess chanted:

'I can count the sands and I can measure the ocean, I have ears for the silent, and know what the dumb man meaneth; Lo! on my sense there strikes the smell of a shell-covered tortoise,

Boiling now on a fire, with the flesh of a lamb, in a cauldron –
Brass is the vessel below, and brass the cover above it.'

Croesus was so impressed by the accuracy of this evidence of second sight that he sent rich gifts to the priestess at Delphi and asked the Oracle what would happen if he attacked Persia. The answer shocked and angered him for the Oracle said that if he embarked on this mad venture he would bring down a mighty empire. He read into it what he wanted, assuming that the empire would be that of Persia. Unfortunately it was his own!

Upton Sinclair

Upton Sinclair, one of the most prolific American writers before and shortly after the First World War, was a pioneer of telepathic research. He and his wife would agree that at certain times when separated by hundreds or even thousands of miles, they would concentrate their thoughts on agreed subjects, and jot them down. Later when they met they compared what they had written and, to the astonishment of both their thoughts coincided in the most remarkable way. This happened frequently when she was in New York and he in California; or when she was in America and he in England. Their experiments in "mental radio" left no doubt in either of their minds that sensitive persons, or those whose minds are suitably attuned, can convey thoughts to each other.

Sir Harry Lauder, the famous comedian, used to say that he was in constant touch, by telepathy, with his brother in New South Wales, Australia; and when Joseph Conrad wanted a book from his library his wife would often go and fetch it without being asked. At first he did not do this consciously but when over an extended period she brought him books he wished to consult at the time, he began willing her to do so. Once his wife dreamt of a cab accident in which he was involved, showing the day and exact time it occurred – and it came to pass.

Sir Gilbert Murray, OM

Gilbert Murray, Professor of Greek at Oxford, was extremely psychic and adept at reading the thoughts of his friends. Maurice Bowra recalled that sometimes he would leave a room while those in it fixed their thoughts on some object or event. He would then be recalled, look round and concentrate for a few moments, after which he would tell them, in a series of steps, what they had thought.

One evening Mrs. Murray, her daughter Rosalind and Bowra took part in an experiment. They agreed to think about the same thing and when Murray came into the room he stated, after a slight pause: 'There's blood in it . . . a crowd shouting . . . it's Paris . . . there's a guillotine . . . it's the execution of Marie Antoinette!' He was right.

On another occasion an experiment was carried out when

Arnold Toynbee, the historian, was present. Murray left the room and Toynbee dictated the following passage into a recorder: 'Isle of Capri, and on it the old Master of Balliol (Strachan Davidson) and my uncle, and they are reading the Bible, and my uncle says what a good book it is, and Strachan Davidson is chuckling.'

Murray was then recalled and his interpretation was also recorded. 'I get someone on the Riviera,' he said; being very funny about the Book of Samuel. He had never read it. It's Italy, I'm sure, and it's about somebody being impressed by the Bible or talking about it as though he had never read it before. I get the name Strachan Davidson. I should say it was at Naples, or at some place with blue sea all about it. Should say it was Capri. Oh, your uncle, Arnold Toynbee.'

That anyone should be able to received such accurate telepathic impressions seems remarkable.

Murray was of Irish descent. His mother was fey and he must have inherited psychic qualities. Bowra says that even in conversation he showed a clairvoyant instinct into what he was thinking and quickly adapted himself to Bowra's moods and their very tone.*

Society For Psychical Research

In 1882 the Society For Psychical Research (SPR) was founded to investigate every kind of supernormal phenomena and the phrase "thought transference" was coined by Frederic Myers, an Inspector of Schools, who devoted a great deal of time, and £700 a year, to find out exactly what ESP is. The phrase "thought transference" was later substituted by "telepathy," and of the first 20 parts of the *Proceedings* of the Society no fewer than 15 contained reports or papers on telepathy. Soon the word was used by investigators to explain such phenomena as could otherwise have been established by spirit communication.

For years most scientists have been extremely sceptical and refused to believe that some people could project their thoughts or receive the thoughts of others. They put it down to trickery, but Cambridge University, so often in the van in such matters, awarded an MD degree in 1946 to L. V. Bendit for his thesis on

Memories: C. M. Bowra

Paracognition, which included telepathy and second sight. Bendit's wife was clairvoyant and his thesis largely concerned her special gift.

The Amazing Harold Sherman

In 1937 Soviet two fliers astonished the world by flying to the United States by way of the North Pole and Alaska. A third flight by Sigismund Lavenesky ended in disaster, his plane being forced down about 450 miles on the American side between the 82nd and 83rd parallels north of Alaska.

As at the time Russia had no equipment with which to conduct the search, the Soviet Government asked Sir Hubert Wilkins the Arctic explorer, to try to find them and provided him with a specially equipped plane. Wilkins established his headquarters at Alkavik near the mouth of the Mackenzie River, about 3,000 miles north of New York. Though Wilkins had a short wave transmitter the conditions were so bad that he was unable to keep in touch with civilization and only on 13 occasions did his messages get through.

Wilkins was interested in telepathy so before leaving New York he arranged with Harold Sherman whom he had met off and on for some years, that he would send him telepathic messages on three days of each week at about 10.30 p.m., for Sherman was a noted telepathic instrument.

Unfortunately because he had so much to do, Wilkins was not always able to concentrate and send out telepathic messages at the times arranged, which makes the result of their experiment all the more remarkable. He tried his utmost to concentrate, however, and send messages, copies of which were made by Dr. Gardner Murphy, the American psychologist and a prominent member of the American SPR. One copy was always sent to Wilkins. They arrived in batches and Sir Hubert compared them with the notes he made when sending them out. All these are continued in a book written by Sherman.

On 22nd October he left New York for Winnipeg where he intended to pick up essential equipment. He arranged to leave Winnipeg on 11th November and intended to drop a wreath on the city as a tribute to the Canadians who died in the war, but in the bustle of getting away, forgot. The Mayor entertained him to breakfast at 10. a.m. and presented him with a city badge which was pinned on to a lapel by Mrs. Innes Taylor. He was also given the freedom of the city. In his speech Wilkins prophesied that in the next war aircraft would annihilate civil populations and made a plea for the constructive use of the airplane.

Then he set off for Edmonton, the next leg of his journey but bad weather forced him to return and he landed at Regina, where various festivities were in progress and the Mayor persuaded him to attend a ball that evening. As he had brought no evening clothes, an officer who was going in uniform, lent him evening dress.

The telepathic impressions gained by Sherman were startling, it not completely accurate. 'You are at Winnipeg;' he wrote; 'a busy day. You roped in on Armistice observance. Tribute to Canadian war dead. Flowers dropped from plane. Aircraft in next war to annihilate civil population. You in plea for constructive use of airplane. Tribute to fellowship aviators of all nations – fact you are going on expedition to search for Russian fliers – to attempt to do for them as you would wish to be done by. You bemoan loss of fellowship between nations when so great a work to be done by all.

'You in company men in military dress. Some women evening dress – social occasion – important people present. You appear in evening dress yourself. Someone seems to put up or pin something on your coat – either pins or a medal or tokens of some kind. You pleased with charcoal likeness.'

This reference is to a charcoal portrait of Wilkins drawn by Miss Shackleton and published in a Canadian newspaper.

The only inaccuracy was that these events occurred in Regina and not in Winnipeg.

On 15th November the plane was fitted with skis and Sherman, who could not possibly have known, recorded: 'Skis put back. Get third floor impression as though you so located.' Sir Hubert's room was on the third floor of his hotel.

On 23rd November Sherman wrote: 'You made Alkavik in two hops.' This was astonishing as Wilkins intended to fly direct to Alkavik but was forced down at Resolution where he stayed for two days.

Sherman continued to record minor events which no one could have told him about, as for instance, on 27th January, when he wrote: 'A dog seems to have been injured at Alkavik and had to be shot. – quite a strong feeling here.' On that day Wilkins walked along the bank of a river where he came upon the body of a dog – shot through the head.

On 31st January he recorded: 'You seem to have a batch of mail ready to send to Slater. Seem to hear you say to someone: "If radio communication keeps on this bad I'll have to develop telepathic communication with Sherman in order to get anything through.'

On that day Wilkins' diary contained almost the identical words Sherman had written.

There were innumerable impressions recorded by Sherman; and only a few more will suffice to show that telepathic communication is possible. On 15th January Sherman wrote: 'Intense activity preparing to leave Edmonton for Alkavik – you purchase a handful of what appears to me metal washers or rings; see yellow colour . . . wonder if this colour is part of the engine.'

Sherman did not know, in fact, that the engine and all spares were wrapped in yellow waterproof material.

On 17th January Sherman wrote: 'Flight back to Alkavik made successfully . . . new propeller to go with new motor. Seem to see it . . . something about pitch of propeller. Seems as though pitch of both propellers must be the same. I have no technical knowledge and do not know what this means.'

This entry seems incredible as the difference in pitch was so slight that it could not be detected by the naked eye and had to be seen and corrected by a delicate instrument. Yet, Sherman was dead right.

Sherman's entry for 7th March ran: 'Your next flight will be your longest to date – around 1,300 miles out and 1,300 miles back – feel you intend to approach within 150 or 200 miles of the Pole.' Which was precisely what Wilkins did.

And on 14th March, while the plane was in the air, Sherman received this impression: 'Seem to see you manipulating hand pump of some sort in flight – one of the engines emitting black smoke – sharp detonations from motor.' This is exactly what happened. The engine nearly stopped and there was some feverish pumping before she could be made to run normally again.

The Sherman-Wilkins experiment is probably the most detailed and accurate recorded over an extended period and there is no possible way in which it could have been faked.

The Case of Ilga Kripps

In 1936 Harry Price, one of the foremost investigators into the supernatural became interested in Ilga Kripps, a six-year old Latvian child in Riga. He found that when her mother read a letter in one room Ilga could repeat it verbatim, in the next. Price suspected trickery, so Ilga was placed in a steel vault of a bank while her mother read passages from a book selected by independent witnesses, and again she repeated every word without error. When tested later in the sound-proof studios of the Riga broadcasting studios, however, her powers failed. As there was no way in which trickery could have been used in the bank Price was forced to ask himself whether telepathic waves could penetrate some materials and not others, a problem which remains to be solved.

Ruskin's Wife

John Ruskin's wife Severn did not realize that she was psychic till one morning she was awakened with a start. Someone seemed to have hit her violently on the mouth, drawing blood. She sat up in bed and pressed a handkerchief to her lips to staunch the flow of blood before realizing that it had all occurred in a dream. She glanced at the clock, noted that it was seven and thought her husband had gone for an early sail, as was his custom. Then she fell asleep again.

When she came down to breakfast at half past nine her husband, who arrived late, kept putting his handkerchief to his mouth. 'Is there anything the matter, John?' she asked.

'Nothing much,' he explained; 'when I was sailing a sudden squall threw the tiller round and it struck me a blow on the mouth, under the upper lip. It has been bleeding a great deal.'

'What time did it happen?'

'I should say about seven.'

There have been innumerable theories to explain telepathy. Oscar Bagnall the well known biologist, wrote in *Country Life:* 'I have gathered considerable evidence that rays emitted by our bodies have a wave length somewhere in the ultra-violet range – probably just short of our visible range, but within that of nocturnal animals, the retinas of whose eyes are studded with nerve endings not unlike those we use for night-seeing and which are blinded by daylight.' That radiations are emitted by the body has been proved by Dr. Kilner, the Kirlians in Russia, and others.

Bagnall continues: 'It is possible that these bright pencil rays register themselves on the auric fields of others in close proximity to them. I an not suggesting that interference takes place in the waves and, even if it did, I cannot see how the rays that have already left the body – and are travelling away from it – could signal back along their own tracks such interference in the amplitude of their waves. Possibly the increased energy due to the interference may be able to make itself felt on the receiving tissue of another person.

'Since the ultra-violet rays incident upon the body are invisible, the emitted rays must have their wave lengths changed (lengthened) by fluorexcent tissue present somewhere in our bodies, since they have become visible. The nervous tissue certainly seems to be responsible for the emission of those far reaching search-like rays. Could they be a possible agent for thought transmission?'

An interesting theory but one which lacks proof. And how does he account for thoughts being transmitted to people thousands of miles away, over seas and across mountain ranges, unless those who receive the thoughts have an apparatus which accepts rays of precisely the same length? Further research is needed before we know how thoughts are transmitted and received.

A curious incident in which telepathy was involved occurred in France in 1923, where a certain Mme D took her bath at six every evening. One evening after lowering herself into the water an escape of gas from the heater overcame her and after screaming for help she sank back unconscious. Her husband who was in the house, heard her screams, rushed in and lifted her out.

After she had been revived and was convalescing, her husband asked: 'Did you, as drowning people are supposed to do, review the events of your past life just before losing consciousness?'

'No,' she replied; 'my thoughts were not for myself, but I saw before me – I hadn't the power to dispel it – the image of Mme J (a friend of the family) looking at me sadly.'

Next morning they received the sad news that Mme J had been drowned while taking a bath, in an advanced state of intoxication, at six the previous evening.

Thoughts are often unconsciously transmitted to those with whom one has an affinity, or between whom rapport exists. Sometimes when working, a few bars of a tune enter my head and within a few seconds I hear my wife downstairs, or in another room, humming it. I remember visiting her before we were married and as she opened the door, I asked without thinking: 'Mrs. Sullivan's here – isn't she?'

'Yes,' she replied; 'but how did you know?' I had met Mrs. Sullivan once only and that for a few minutes, and had never given her another thought; but my wife had just been talking to her, and her thoughts must have been telepathically transferred to me.

On another occasion, during the war, when rationing was very strict, I looked up from an article I was typing and called: 'Are you going to cook some rice today?' I did not know we had any in the house but suddenly the thought came into my head. Unknown to me, however, my wife had found some at the corner shop.

She came into the room where I was working, looking somewhat startled. 'How did you know? I had my hand on the rice jar just as you spoke.' I didn't know, but she was thinking of rice and her thoughts had been transferred to me. Many husbands and wives must have had similar experiences, which they dismissed as having no significance whatever.

Maurice Barbanell

Maurice Barbanell, Editor of *Psychic News,* is known to all who are interested in ESP. He once wrote a letter to a newspaper in which he said that a friend whose wife regularly practised telepathy would give him a demonstration of her powers. 'When we leave this evening,' he said; 'come and dine with myself and my wife at our Manchester home. I will let her know you are coming.'

'He sat down and concentrated. He was sending his wife a message,' he explained. 'He did not leave my sight from then until we arrived at his Manchester home. His wife greeted me with the comment: "I got your message, Ernest," and took us into the dining room where the table was laid for three; and they were not on the telephone.'*

*Star: 12.6.1951

Few who send or receive telepathic messages can do so at will. For the vast majority messages come out of the blue, and often as warnings.

The Dead Man's Message

Whether the dead can converse coherently with the living is a matter of controversy, for most of the messages relayed from "the other side" by mediums are so footling and puerile that one concludes that the dead must have softening of the brain. There are exceptions. Oliver Moxon received a message from his friend Jim while serving in the Imphal Valley in Burma. Jim had been shot down in his Hurricane a few days earlier. A day or two after Jim failed to return, Moxon heard his voice distinctly, giving the exact location by map reference, of a large Japanese ammunition dump some 20 miles south-east of Kalewa on the Chindwin River.

Next morning by coincidence, they were ordered to strafe a dump 'somewhere about 20 miles south-east of Kalewa.' While the rest of the squadron fired haphazardly into the jungle, Moxon pin-pointed the dump by his map reference, which lay in the middle of a very thick clump of trees. The tremendous explosion after he had fired left no doubt in his mind about the authenticity of the message sent by Jim.

Telepathy Enabled Them To Escape

Mr. C. Gordon of Bexley, a bombardier during the 1939 war, was captured with another member of his regiment and marched up a quiet road by an escort of two armed Germans close behind. They were warned that conversation was *verboten* and each time they glanced at each other were prodded by bayonets. After covering some miles Gordon felt a message clarifying in his mind which seemed to say 'We must escape.' It grew stronger and stronger till the word 'Now' flashed into his mind. He also sensed that his friend had received the same message, so turned and attacked the guard behind him. His friend simultaneously made an attack and the Germans, taken by surprise, were knocked to the ground before they could take action. Within minutes, rifles in their hands, the Britons were across the fields and on their way to freedom. Had both not received the same message at the same time they would not have acted in concert and would have been killed.

A Delirious Mind

As stated earlier illness often makes the mind more acute and sensitive than it is in health. This was so in the case of Bryan Morton of Bristol, who in 1943 lay dangerously ill in an Italian hospital. The nurses told him later that he had grown delirious and imagined he was floating in the sky over Italy.

He remembers that he saw an old friend in a Spitfire on patrol and, coming up fast behind was a Messerschmidt. He half rose and called out: 'Look out, Derek – he's on your tail!' at which his friend swerved into a bank of cloud.

A week later he received a letter from his friend, which ran: 'Yesterday I had the most extraordinary experience. I was stooging about on patrol over S........when I heard your voice say: 'Look out Derek – he's on your tail!' I went into a quick climbing turn and sure enough there was a 109. Instead of him getting me, I got him. Except for that hallucination I'd have been a goner.' That was not hallucination but a telepathic message.

When Hitler Marched Into Prague

Constant danger also makes the mind more sensitive and in this state a sixth sense predominates. Mr. F. J. Weale, a Czech, left Prague on 14th March 1939, leaving his family behind. He informed his wife that he intended to travel to Geneva where she arranged to follow him within the next few days. The next day, however, Hitler marched into Prague and the Bohemian frontiers were closed.

By then Weale was in Paris and because the situation had changed, decided to make for London instead of Geneva. He was worried nearly out of his mind because he knew that the safety of his wife and family would be at risk if he phoned Prague.

He had three hours to wait before the train to Calais pulled out when something forced him in the direction of a hotel in which he and his wife usually stayed when they visited Paris. 'At the very moment I passed the hotel entrance,' he relates; 'the porter, who knew me, but had not expected me that day, came running out, obviously looking for someone.

' "Mr. Weale," he shouted on spotting me; "You are wanted on the telephone." ' It was a call from his wife in Prague.

Although she knew he should have been in Geneva, a voice told her that he was in Paris and at the hotel in which they usually stayed. Events such as this seem to rule out coincidence.

Constant danger undoubtedly hones the sixth sense. Col. Jim Corbett wrote:* 'I have made mention elsewhere of the sense that warns us of impending danger . . . this sense is a very real one, and I do not know, and therefore cannot explain, what brings it into operation. On this occasion I had neither heard nor seen the tigress, nor had I received any indication from bird or beast of her presence, and yet I knew, without any shadow of doubt, that she was lying up for me among the rocks. I had been out for many hours that day and had covered many miles of jungle with unflagging caution, but without one moment's unease, and then, on cresting the ridge, and coming in sight of the rocks, I knew they held danger for me, and this knowledge was confirmed a few minutes later by the kakar's warning call to the jungle folk, and by finding the man-eater's pug marks superimposed on my footprints.'

She knows When Her Husband Is Returning Home

Mrs. Young, whose husband was Vicar of Kensworth, Beds, almost invariably knew when her husband, who was often kept late by his duties, would return. 'One evening,' she says; 'I was eating my supper when I heard, as I thought, my husband come in.

'I quickly turned up the light under the kettle and waited, expecting to hear my husband's voice. Minutes passed and at last I went to the door and called him but there was no answer. There was no one else in the house. Exactly 15 minutes later he did return and we judged that at the time of my experience he was thinking intently of his home coming.

'This has happened so often that when my husband is out I now wait for the premonition before I put the kettle on.'

His father Called Him

When Mr. R. Gilbert of Harlington, Middlesex, was 12 he

Man-Eaters of Kumaon: Jim Corbett

stayed with relatives in a country house on a mountain in Austria, the only path to the place being through a dense wood. One evening he had a strong feeling that his father was in the wood, calling to him, which was strange because he was expected to travel from Vienna the following day. As the feeling grew stronger he became so agitated that his cousins, to humour him said they would look for his father and he begged to be allowed to accompany them.

He led the way, calling 'Papa! Papa! 'but after covering about a mile and a half they decided to abandon the search. As they turned they received an answering call and to their surprise found Mr. Gilbert a short distance away. He had decided to travel a day earlier and on his way through the wood tripped over a tree trunk and injured an ankle so badly that he could not walk. After falling he called his son's name repeatedly – and though a long way off, his thoughts had carried.

The Colonel's Premonition

Between the wars Mrs. Mawson, whose husband was stationed in Singapore, arranged with four friends to hold a charity dance, and it was agreed that she should try to obtain the services of an Indian regimental band.

The following Sunday during tea, her mother said: 'We are not going to church.' At the same time she got a mental picture of herself meeting the Colonel of the Indian regiment at the cathedral door, and getting permission to have the use of the band. So she answered: 'I have to go to church, Mother; may I have the Victoria?' Her mother agreed.

On her arrival at the cathedral the Colonel came forward unexpectedly and helped her to alight. He said that he and his family had not intended to be at the evening service but he had changed his mind because he had a premonition that Mrs. Mawson would be there to ask a favour of him.

'What is it that your mother wants me to do?' he asked. She told him, and in the circumstances he could hardly have refused. This seems a case in which both parties have the same thoughts passing between them.

A Dying Mother's Thoughts

When death is imminent the power of thought sometimes grows

stronger. In 1938 when Mr. P. J. Devlin was living in Secunderabad, India, his mother fell ill and was taken to hospital. He says: 'I received a tempting offer to go to Bombay and drive a new car for the firm's car dealers. I accepted, told my mother I would be away only a few days, and set off. I reached Poona where I had to change trains, but instead of continuing to Bombay I took the next train back to Secunderabad.

'I don't know why I did this but on reaching Secunderabad I went straight to the hospital and found my mother was sinking fast. She died that afternoon.' Not before he had spoken to her, however, for her thoughts as life ebbed from her were focussed powerfully on her son and forced him to return instead of going on to Bombay. Thoughts, if concentrated powerfully enough, can affect and influence others even though they be thousands of miles away.

Depressed By Thoughts

On 4th April 1943 Mrs. Narraway, whose son was serving on "HMS Dorsetshire" somewhere in the Far East, woke while still very drowsy, which was most unusual, and had to force herself to get up.

'As the day went on,' she recalled; 'I still felt very drowsy but managed to cook dinner for myself and the younger members of my family though the children said they were not in the least bit hungry.' This was most unusual for, like most healthy children they had appetites like wolves.

Then news came through on the radio that the "Dorsetshire" had been sunk in the Indian Ocean, her crew being picked up after 48 hours in the water. 'My son,' says Mrs. Narraway,' was a survivor and it turned out that we were all very depressed while he was in the water.'

The mutual feeling may have been coincidental but it may also have been caused by the father's thoughts which were concentrated powerfully on his family, and though two continents apart these were impinged powerfully on their consciousness. Many cases of depression may be caused by thought waves sent out by relatives we love, who are in pain or anguish.

Often when your thoughts are concentrated on one particular person, he, too, may be thinking about you. Most of us have at some time picked up a telephone to ring a friend and then hear him say: 'How odd! I was just about to ring you.;' or, 'I've been thinking about you for some time and was about to get in touch.' It must happen to hundreds each week, though they fail to record such trivial events.

Mr. Elton's Message

One who recorded just such an event was Mr. Elton, an insurance inspector, who specialized in selling sickness and accident insurance to professional men.

'One morning in 1923,' he wrote; 'while on my way to Broad Street, E.C. London, I felt impelled to retrace my steps and go to Walbrook.

'I did so and entered the first building I reached and told the liftman to take me to the third floor. There I found the door of an office opposite the lift open and inside was a chartered accountant to whom I handed my card. He hardly glanced at it but expressed astonishment that I had come so promptly considering it was barely 20 minutes since he had phoned my company asking them to send an inspector to arrange sickness and accident insurance for them.

'When I pointed out that I had not come from the company he mentioned and told him the extraordinary circumstances which brought me to him, he was so astonished that he decided to give me the business.'

What force compelled Mr. Elton to change his mind and go to Walbrook when he was on his way to Broad Street? Why had he asked the liftman to take him the third and not the second or the fourth floor? Why had he entered the office opposite the lift? Finally, why had the accountant's thoughts impinged so powerfully on his mind and not on that of the inspector he has asked to see? There is no logical explanation except that on that particular morning their thoughts functioned on the same wave length.

Feelings Defy Logic

Thoughts can be so powerful that sometimes they arouse emotions in others and make them act in ways they would not otherwise do. Mr. L. Momikos says: 'I was born in Greece and left during the occupation (by the Nazis) for South Africa. A month after the liberation of Greece we were on our way to

Egypt by plane.

'The night before our arrival in Egypt I had a funny sensation that my uncle and his family would be waiting for us at the aerodrome. I told my father, who replied: 'Nonsense! Your uncle is in Greece and not likely to go to Egypt as he has no interests there.

'On our arrival in Egypt, however, we found my uncle and his family waiting for us just as I had imagined it.' How can one explain that except by accepting that there must have been a telepathic influence?

Pain Transmission By Thought

Pain is often transmitted by thought as thousands of men must realize when their wives are giving birth. Mr. Geoffrey L. Jeff of Haslemere, Surrey, took a walking-cum-camping holiday in County Wicklow with an old friend and one evening camped on the mountainside overlooking Glendaloch.

'My friend,' says Jeff; 'set off for the village in the valley three miles below for post and provisions. About 30 minutes after he left I felt strangely disturbed. My right leg became very painful, but I could stand.

'I felt a sudden urge to follow my friend and on my way down I heard a low moan. I found my friend lying unconscious and it was then that I realized that my previous discomfort had now disappeared.

'Some loose boulders, dislodged as he slid down, had overtaken him and he was pinned with his right leg against a tree stump by a large piece of rock.'

As the two were close friends with much in common, some form of empathy existed between them and the pain felt by his friend was transmitted by thought waves to Mr. Jeff, in precisely the same place as his injury.

He Knew When A Message Came Through

Years ago Mr. M. A. Sauvage of Grosvenor Hill, S.W.19 lived in a town where the local doctor was a great friend. One night he woke from a deep sleep with the feeling that he had received an urgent call. 'I rose,' he said; 'and went to the window and to my astonishment my friend, the doctor, drove past and waved to me.

129

'Later he said that on receiving this call he had tried to send me a message by telepathy. From then on, whenever he was called out at night he sent me a message which I never failed to receive.

'Sometimes I would telephone him at his surgery, always sending him a "message" about two minutes before lifting the receiver. Of all the calls coming into his surgery he always knew when to tell his secretary that it was a private call which he would answer himself.'

This is a remarkable example of telepathic communication between people with a strong bond of friendship, almost as if a telephone link existed between them. This usually happens in the case of identical twins.

Identical Twins

Identical twins are usually born within minutes of each other and in this respect differ from ordinary twins, who may be born hours, weeks and even months apart. There is a case in Australia of twins being born nearly two months apart and, at the Motala Municipal Maternity Hospital, Sweden, of twins being born three months apart!

Identical twins are born so close together that almost invariably they look alike and have the same characteristics, habits, abilities and thoughts. Because of this they can communicate with each other though separated by oceans. The twins Elfriede and Auguste Sejvel of Vienna, had the same tastes, voice tones, heart-beat and blood pressure. They were always the same weight and their finger prints were identical, the odds against which are 64,000,000,000 to one!

The famous Bedser twins look so alike that even close friends were often baffled. Their careers followed the same pattern and when they retired from cricket they went into the same business as partners. They thought alike and knew at any given moment what the other was going to do.

Jean and Jo Readinger, American twins who came from America to dance at the Mayfair Hotel in London in 1937 were so alike that they made the same dancing mistakes at the same time and if one fell, the other fell, too. One always knew what the other was thinking, so they decided to put it to the test. One accepted a job in Chicago and the other in Pittsburg, 600 miles apart. One night Jo invented a new dance step and worked on it

130

till she was perfect. When they met a week later they found that each had thought of the same steps, which were intricate and original. Letters they wrote to each other contained identical incidents which had happened to both. There are scores of similar cases vouched for by medical men, which proves that telepathic communication takes place between identical twins.

A Penny For Your Thoughts

When one is pensive and lost in thought friends sometimes say: 'A penny for your thoughts.' This is what happened to A. W. H. Rickard of Bromley, Kent. It happened on 3rd July 1915, his 28th birthday, when he was guarding the pipeline on the Persian frontier, with eight Pathans, none of whom knew a word of English.

As he had not been home for eight years Rickard was thinking: 'I wonder how many more birthdays will pass before I see my folks agin.' Then he noticed one of his men looking intently at him. Suddenly he spoke in Pushtu, which when translated, ran: 'This time next year, Sahib, you will be in England – and married.'

Rickard laughed. He knew no girls in England, and in any case, it was his intention to return to the North-West Frontier in India when the war was over, and carry on in the Frontier Police.

But the Pathan knew better. Three weeks later Rickard was wounded and invalided home. In November he met a girl whom he married on 26th June – a week under a year – just as the Pathan had "seen." How did he know? One can understand his reading of Rickard's thoughts but how did he see what would happen in the future? If that is possible the potentialities of the mind are unlimited.

Dr. Mak Ting Sum

Dr. Mak Ting Sum who lived at 12, Jalan Skela, Kuala Lumpur, Malaysia, was famous throughout South-East Asia for his powers of healing by telepathy. On 26th December 1956 the *Malay Mail* carried a feature about him which advised physicians, scientists and thinkers to investigate his powers and co-operate with him. In the *Week-Ender* of 13th May 1955, another Malaysian periodical, Jeffrey Francis wrote an article entitled "The Strange Powers of Dr. Mak," in which he stated that the Doctor also helps to mend broken marriages, students who have difficulty in passing examinations, and traces missing persons – all by telepathy.

In February 1959 Mr. Alfred Mills, D.MS., a student of metaphysics who was doing research into ESP, tested Dr. Mak's powers. He suffered from severe pains in his chest and after consultation Dr. Mak told him that the cure would start the following morning. Mills retired to bed on 4th March and woke at 6.30 (his normal time of waking was 7.30) with a sharp pain in his chest and a feeling of nausea. Minutes later, while dressing, pain and nausea vanished as suddenly as they had come on. On subsequent mornings he woke at 6.30 which he had rarely done in the past, and pain and nausea were less on each occasion. Eventually they disappeared and he found to his astonishment that the telepathic treatment had worked!

Incidentally, Dr. Mak is a scientist, a Ph.D., a Doctor of Mechano-therapy and Suggested Therapeutics, a Fellow of the International Association of Masso-Therapists, a Fellow of the London College of Physiology, and a Member of the Societie Internationale Pilogogie Sciences.

Science Tries to Harness Telepathy

Harold Sherman, who has spent half a lifetime in experiments with telepathy, says: 'I believe that various phases of ESP, catalogued as telepathy, clairvoyance, clairaudience, psychokinesis, precognition, trance mediumship, poltergeist, psychometry and the like, *are all parts of one whole*.

'If I am right in this conviction, then a true sensitive should be able eventually to manifest ESP ability in all these "psychic areas."

'We know there is something in the mind which can move backward and forward in time. Unhappily we have developed the concept that we are physically in one place and cannot be in any other. This concept inhibits the ability in our ESP faculties to move unrestrictedly in time and space.

'Occasionally, however, something happens and we find that we have moved ahead in time and have been given a precognitive glimpse of an event coming towards us, *in time*.'

Dr. Reiser

Dr. Oliver Reiser, Professor of Philosophy at the University of Pittsburg, propounded the theory that we are not finished products of evolution but are in the process of acquiring new and startling talents, among them clairvoyance, telepathy and extra-sensory perceptions. We are becoming increasingly able to perceive things by thought waves sent out by one mind to another.

'If,' he says; 'like some neurologists, we may believe that the brain is not yet a fulfilled product but at present merely represents an intermediate state of evolution, we have a possible biological basis for the doctrine that still higher functions remain to be solved. Thus, we might hopefully suppose that a great composite being is beginning to emerge and reveal its form in the extra-sensory perceptions which today appear as but feeble and flickering imitations of psychic powers yet to be developed.

'Does thought exist for the purpose of guiding or changing our actions or does human action proceed according to physiological patterns of which "thought" is merely a just-ification?"

Dr. Gustav Stromberg

Dr. Gustav Stromberg, an astro-physicist at the Carnegie Institute, who has been thinking along similar lines, advances a theory to explain psychic phenomena. 'Behind the world of phenomena,' he says; 'we perceive with our sense organs that there is another world to which we cannot apply ordinary concepts of space and time. The particles of matter, the elements which determine the growth, structures, and the functions in living organisms, as well as the nerves in our nervous system and our brain, which make possible our sensations, feelings, memories and thoughts – all have their "roots" in a world beyond space and time.

'It is thus no longer so difficult to understand that the thoughts in the mind of one individual can directly influence the thoughts of another. The minds of all people have a common origin and the elements in our brains which are responsible for mental activities have never lost their connection with their ultimate source.'

These connecting links, explains Stromberg, are not physical but of a more subtle type, for they do not consist of particles or electromagnetic waves; and since they are not physical they have no size and their effect does not decrease with distance or take a finite time for transmission.

To grasp this we must rid ourselves of preconceived theories built on purely physical science which says, for instance, that the same thing cannot be in two different places at the same time, a condition known as bilocation. In the past some famous people have been seen in two places some hundreds of miles apart, at the same time, but scientists have scoffed at the observers and said they were subject to hallucinations. It may also be possible for the same event to be observed simultaneously at two different points miles distant from each other. And the preconceived notion that in order to get from one place to another it is necessary to travel through intervening space must also be abolished; or that it takes time to accomplish this. According to Dr. Reiser it can happen instantly.

All this may seem fantastic nonsense but we exist in a world in which the seemingly impossible has come to pass: where men travel to the moon, defying the laws of gravity; and inter-planetary travel, where bodies become weightless and limbs refuse to obey the dictates of the mind.

Dr. Franz J. Polgar

The case of Dr. Franz J. Polgar, a Hungarian lieutenant during the First World War, is probably unique. During a heavy bombardment he was knocked unconscious and taken to the nearest hospital. On regaining consciousness he found he could read the thoughts of the nurses and doctors around him, and told them what they were thinking. They tested him again and again and in due course reported their findings to German Intelligence, who decided to exploit his unusual talent. Unfortunately for them their treatment of their Hungarian allies had so embittered Dr. Polgar that when asked to read the thoughts of captured Allied prisoners in order to gain information about troop movements he suddenly found he had "lost" the ability to read thoughts.

After the war he emigrated to America and at New York University, where he was employed, again demonstrated his

134

thought-reading ability. He was investigated by dozens of learned societies and in every instance found to be genuine. What eventually became of him is not known, for disliking the Germans as he did, he would have been invaluable to America in the Second World War in probing the minds of prisoners.

There is increasing interest in telepathy among scientists the world over, especially those in Russia and America, who are trying to harness it in order to communicate with space travellers, and in war. During the International Astronautical Congress in Paris in 1963 the American delates discussed thought transference seriously and Dr. Eugene Konecci, Director of Biotechnology and Human Research of NASA, the American Space Agency, said: 'If the results of conducted experiments are half as good as the Soviets claim, then they may be the first to put a human thought into orbit, or to achieve mind-to-mind communication with humans on the moon,' for at that time the Russians had eight centres devoted to studying the problems of telepathic communication on a scientific basis.

The Americans are not lagging for their space project, known as PIAPACS (Psycho-physiological information, acquisition, processing and control systems), is also engrossed in this work. Both countries are pouring money and effort into these projects and giving them high priority.

Work At Hanscomb Field

In 1962 a research team consisting of a psychologist, a physicist, an electronics engineer and a mathematician, built a computer to test telepathy, clairvoyance and precognition at Hanscomb Field, Bedford, Massachusetts. They enlisted the aid of girls from Endicott Junior College, Beverly because it was thought that female intuition has something in common with ESP.

Hanscomb Field is the headquarters of the electronics systems division of the US Air Force and the USAF Cambridge Research Laboratories are situated there. Eventually a report was published in which it was suggested that they had taken a new direction by employing automatic equipment to eliminate human bias and error. But Dr. Stephen I. Abrams, an American engaged in research into parapsychology at Oxford University, said that their report veered on the optimistic, adding however, that the real significance lay in the fact that the

USAF was putting so much effort and money into such a nebulous project and was prepared to publicize it, for at least one member of the team was an astro-physicist.

Testing Telepathy Over Distance

In 1964 a British experiment was launched between London and Athens. Mr. S. D. Cornell of Cambridge University Psychical Research went to Greece to arrange details of the experiment with Admiral Tanagarus, head of the Greek Society for Psychical Research. Mr. Cornell said he thought there was enough evidence to establish that telepathy was a fact, but no one had any idea which part of the brain was involved, or what caused it. His experiment was mainly to find out whether telepathic impressions weakened with distance. The Russians believe that telepathy uses electromagnetic waves which weaken with distance and Mr. Cornell is inclined to agree; but he added that some of their published data was very bad and points to them not being certain of themselves.

The experiment between London and Athens involved hypnotised and unhypnotised subjects who transmitted impressions about visible and imagined subjects, and zener cards. 'The experiment,' Dr. Cornell added; 'may be a complete waste of time. An experiment between Cambridge and Chicago four years ago produced insignificant results, with nothing that was not due to chance . . . but in this subject one must try all manner of things.'

Dr. Stephen I. Abrams

That the leading British universities take ESP in general and telepathy in particular, seriously, is shown by the award of the Perrott-Warrick studentship in psychical research at Trinity College, Cambridge, to Dr. Stephen I. Abrams, an American research student at St. Catherine's College, Oxford. Dr. Abrams was a Fellow in parapsychology at Duke University, USA in 1958 and 1959; visiting lecturer at the CG Jung-Institut in Zurich in 1959, and in 1962 the first western scientist to visit Soviet ESP centres, where he lectured at Leningrad University and the Neurophysiology Institute of the Moscow Academy of Sciences.

Dr. Abrams, who was attached to the Unit of Biometry in

Oxford, is reported to have said: 'It's unfortunate that our students have less tolerance for new ideas than their Russian colleagues . . . If we can harness telepathy what new realms may not be explored!'

Experiments of Professor L. L. Vasiliev

The Russians evidently do not subscribe to the theory that telepathic waves weaken with distance. Dr. L. L. Vasiliev, Professor of Physiology at Leningrad University, stated that hundreds of Soviet tests tend to discredit the theory that telepathy works by electromagnetic impulses transmitted by the brain. He started his experiments in 1921 under the direction of Dr. V. M. Bechterov and in 1937 when he was Director, it became clear that 'mental influencing was a reality and that it was not impeded by electromagnetic radiation.' As he could advance no reason for telepathic communication, however, the authorities ordered him to stop research; but in 1959 reports filtered through that the Americans were interested in the subject, and work was continued. His book gives details of his experiments during the twenties and thirties and links these with experiments carried out on the US nuclear submarine "Nautilus" in 1959. He says: 'This experiment shows that telepathic information can be transmitted without loss through a thickness of sea water and through the sealed metal covering of a submarine; that is, through substances which greatly interfere with radio communication.'

Vasiliev makes no claims, saying modestly that 'Every year more and more researchers are being convinced of the real existence of mental suggestion, and the study of various aspects of these complex phenomena.'

Proof, he suggested, was not always necessary; the existence of the phenomenon was often enough, for proof could come later. 'Let us recall the discovery of the meson field,' he said; 'which was neglected at first and only experimentally confirmed after ten years'. Of course, everything that exists in the universe is not as yet fully understood.

'Now micro-fields are being discovered not exceeding the boundaries of the atom; could one not suppose that sooner or later a new micro-field will be discovered which will go beyond the boundaries of atoms and engulf the surrounding space?'

137

Some scientists are already working on research to prove that a gravitational field seems to have a similarity with the force which transmits telepathic information, acting at a distance and penetrating all obstacles.

Russian Experiments In Telepathy

In 1966 "Komsomolskaya Pravda," the newspaper of the Young Communist League, reported an experiment in telepathy organised by Dr. I. M. Kogan, which took place between researchers 2,000 miles apart, The "transmitter" was Yury Kamensky, who sat in a Moscow office, thinking hard on six objects in front of him, while Karl Nikolayev in Novosibirsk concentrated on "receiving" the pictures and putting them down on paper. Among those objects which were identical on Kamensky's table were a coil spring and a coffee pot, while all the others bore reasonable resemblances. He also "saw" correctly 12 out of 25 zener cards transmitted by thought. It is hoped that eventually men will so develop their minds that telepathic messages will be sent and received accurately.

Miss Celia Green, director of the Psychophysical Research Unit at Oxford, said that she and her colleagues were convinced that their research would have far reaching implications in such varied studies as mental health and the nature and time of dreams.

William James

For centuries Man has tried to unravel the mysteries of the mind: what it is; how it works; and why? We are almost as far off as milleniums ago. William James (1842–1910) the American philosopher, suggested that we live immersed in 'a continuum of cosmic consciousness,' a worldly mind which filters into every particular brain and is experienced by the owner of that brain as his private mind or consciousness;' but that fails to explain why some are able to utilise this cosmic consciousness and other are not.

Henry Bergson (1859–1941)

Bergson, the empiricist philosopher, said that the mind is aware of everything, everywhere, without regard to time or space, but that this vast store of information is much too large for one mind to cope with, so in the interests of biological efficiency, much of this is shut out. PSI is merely a leakage into the personal consciousness of some of this material. Bergson emphasised the point that intuition is a reaction or protest against intellect (or intelligence), and its product, science. Intellectual knowledge is what one hears, sees, etc., and is relative knowledge. The intellect is unable fully to understand life, and that is where intuition is so important.

One can cite scores of examples of men of outstanding mental equipment who failed hopelessly when it came to dealing with people and human problems: men with double-firsts from their universities, who towered above their contemporaries. Outside their narrow intellectual fields they fell flat on their faces.

A prime example was Lord Simon, who became Lord Chancellor and was one of the foremost lawyers of his day. He could grasp the technicalities of almost any subject and possessed an astonishingly retentive memory. Yet, he lacked intuition and with it the humanity so essential to dealing with human and international problems, and he was a complete failure outside his particular sphere. He was so pedantic that someone who knew him well said: 'He has descended from a line of maiden aunts.'

Bergson said that total reality is living; that life is reality behind matter; and if everything that has life in it must be known by intuition, then nothing can be fully known unless also known intuitively. It is a means of perceiving whatever can be the object of "sympathetic intelligence," which is, perhaps, the pulse of the earth.

Success In Life Depends On Intuition

Einstein said: 'The great adventure of Man's conquest over his ignorance must rest on artistic intuition and truths demonstrated by the deductive reasoning of great minds . . . For while our knowledge advances by the discovery of new facts, the outstanding landmarks in the progress of science have come from the discovery of natural laws by theoretical explorations of the mind.'

Many great inventions; many exciting plots; many great poems and paintings, have flowered from imagination, inspiration and intuition, all of which are closely related and are components of PSI.

Dr. Elsie Toms

William James's explanation may be the answer to the sort of telepathy experienced by Dr. Elsie Toms of St. Albans, Herts, who wrote: 'Many years ago my mother and I found that we were telepathic and we used that power regularly in perhaps the most matter-of-fact way possible. I did most of the family shopping on Saturday mornings, armed with a shopping list supplied by my mother, and it was quite normal for me to recognise in the middle of a busy street market that my mother had omitted some item.

'I would buy it and bring it home to be told that she had remembered it while I was out and had passed the message to me.

'While I was young news of a success came to me at college though it was not expected for another week. I managed to get a moment's solitude to try to pass the good news to my mother. She was waiting at the window to meet me and her first words before I could speak, were to congratulate me.'*

This seems an exceedingly practical use of telepathy, denied to most mortals.

Mr. and Mrs. Leslie Wilson

Mr. and Mrs. Leslie Wilson, of Worple Road, Wimbledon, also possessed the curious faculty of being able to read each other's thoughts, and often carried out long conversations at a distance without a word being spoken. They were tested by doctors and psychologists, were placed in separate rooms and in different houses, but nothing interfered with the transfer of their thoughts to each other, on the most varied subjects. No explanation could be found.

Mr. Wilson explained: 'I do not really mind about my wife reading my thoughts; in fact, I taught her the art. It is useful, for when the idea of a row is growing in her mind, I know, and can think so as to stop it.' A very useful ability.

Mr. Wilson also possessed the power of deep concentration

*Sun: 27.3.1968

140

and at first when he explained it to his wife, she scoffed; eventually, however, she realized it was true and also mastered the art. In one experiment Mr. Wilson dispatched his wife to a room at the farthest end of the house while a stranger wrote down six names, five living and one dead. He transferred the names telepathically to his wife, and she named the one who was dead – and said so. The other five were correct.

The ability of one spouse to read the thoughts of another can prove an embarrassment, for if thoughts are no longer private, what else is? This may have suited the Wilsons but if the faculty were developed universally it could result in shattered marriages and the divorce rate would rocket, for most married people indulge in trifling (and not so trifling) infidelities from time to time.

The Imposition Of The Will

In 1930 John England, a well known journalist, wrote that he stayed in a country village with the rector, who claimed that he had the power of inflicting his will, at a distance, on others; and by conscious effort he could communicate his wishes to them.

A test was suggested and a professional singer who was a guest, agreed to take part. She was then locked in an upstairs room, after which the Rector wrote five suggestions on slips of paper, describing what he had mentally asked the singer to do. These were shown to the company, none of whom left the room.

On the first slip was written: 'She will come downstairs, stand in the doorway, and sing Stainer's Sevenfold Amen (the Dresden Amen),'

As soon as she appeared she stood in the doorway and sang that florious air. The other four suggestions were also carried out to the letter.*

The Case of Captain MacGowan

The *Journals* of the SPR (Society For Psychical Research) contain scores of substantiated examples of telepathy but one will be sufficient as it was vouched for by Sir William Barrett, FRS.

He said that Captain A. B. MacGowan, an officer in the

*Sunday Mercury & Sunday News. 12.10.1930

American Army, then on leave in Brooklyn, promised his two sons who were on holiday, to take them to the theatre, and booked seats for three. While booking the seats he went into the theatre and examined the interior carefully. As he moved about the place a voice within him kept saying: 'Do not go to the theatre. Take the boys back to school.' The voice continued to nag him on the day of their proposed visit and grew so insistent that he told the boys he had cancelled their visit and they would have to return to school. Friends remonstrated and said it would be cruel to deprive them of their promised treat and he partly relented. But that afternoon he again heard the words so loud and clear that he took his sons back to New York and booked in at a hotel near the station. All three spent a miserable evening and he felt ashamed of breaking his promise.

As he came down to breakfast next morning and picked up his newspaper, the headlines informed him that the theatre they had intended to visit was now a charred ruin. It had been destroyed by one of the worst fires known and 300 of the audience had lost their lives!

Whose voice had warned him? From where had it come, and why were none of the others forewarned?

Telekinesis

We regard the mind as a nebulous entity, without form and containing no matter; but it has now been proved that the mind is a force that can bend objects and move them at will. We call the power which performs such apparent miracles *telekinesis*, a term employed in psychical research for the movement of objects by, and in the presence of, some medium, apparently without contact, and as the result of occult forces. Anything we fail to understand is termed occult! The mind is an occult force. Some yogis have demonstrated telekinesis but as they are indifferent to scientific opinion or public acclaim, have consistently refused to submit to tests. In 1966 Dr. Ctibor Veseley, a lecturer in electro-physiology at the Dradec Kravove University, Czechoslovakia, carried out a number of experiments on an apparatus built by Jiri Macku, the department's engineer. This consisted of a paper-thin copper disc balanced on a needle on which it can be revolved by an electric motor. The apparatus is housed in a glass-sided non-magnetic case.

Sitting six feet from it and concentrating his gaze on the disc,

Robert Pavlita can make it revolve either clockwise or counter-clockwise, slow it down or make it stop. He also has the ability to move light objects floating on water in a predetermined direction by concentrating his will on them. Scores of similar experiments are being carried out, some in collaboration with Russian scientists, in order to discover why objects respond to will power and whether this ability can be developed to move larger and heavier objects at greater distances.

Even more extra-ordinary is the power exerted by Mrs. Mikhailova, a Russian who has only to concentrate her gaze on objects to make them move. Under strict tests she exerts PH (telekinesis) over objects placed under glass cases. Once while dining she concentrated on a piece of bread, which moved towards her in jerks, then she bent and opened her mouth and the bread leapt into it! An egg was placed in a saline solution. She stood six feet away, gazed at it and the yolk separated from the white. Another look and she put them together again. All this with a camera focussed on her.

Yogis have demonstrated publicly in daylight that they can raise objects off the ground by will power alone. Birgitte Valanne, wife of a Finnish diplomat in India, wrote: 'On one occasion, in one of the guest houses of the Birla temples, I saw a holy man lift a chair merely by will power. He asked us to assist him by using our will power; then gazed intently on the chair, which raised itself about two feet into the air, after which it fell to the floor with a crash.'*

Mrs. Valanne also said that when a fakir (yogi) was given a brick, he touched and changed it into sugar before their gaze! The feat could not have been accomplished by hypnotism because she still has a piece of the brick. And part of the factory mark is on it. She also saw an aluminium spoon changed into gold. How useful that power would be to the Chancellor of the Exchequer in balancing the nation's books.

Sir Humphrey Trevelyan

The mind possesses infinite power if only we knew how to use it, as apparently some in the East and in Africa do. By the time one acquires such power, however, one realizes the futility of material possessions. Sir Humphrey Trevelyan says that one

*In Love With India: Birgitte Valanne

evening after dinner at the house of a wealthy landowner named Bertie Ffoulkes, in Madras, a party of Muslim devotees gave a performance in honour of their local saint. While drummers strummed a complicated rhythm, presumably to attain the required vibrations, they stuck long needles through their cheeks and the flesh of their stomachs, without producing a drop of blood. Then, they gouged out their eyeballs with heavy spikes and, as the throbbing of the drums rose to a cresendo, a spike was driven through a young devotee's skull. This, which could be pulled out only by one of them placing a leg against the young man's shoulder and giving a violent tug, leaving a large hole. After this postprandial exercise the performers were restored to health and seemed not one whit the worse. Sir Humphrey gives no explanation, but similar apparent "miracles" have been observed and vouched for by officials and medical men in Asia and Africa over the centuries.

Eight Major Siddhis

The yogis explain that these and other powers can be acquired by mastering the Eight *Siddhis*, which are part of Kundalini Yoga. *Anima* enables a man to become as minute as he pleases; *Mahima* enables him to magnify his body infinitely; by *Laghima* he can become as light as a feather and travel faster than the speed of light; *Gharima* increases his specific gravity; *Prapti* gives him the power of clairvoyance, clairaudience, telepathy and thought-reading; the ability to cure all disease and to understand the language of birds and animals; *Prakamya* enables him to submerge indefinitely under water; Vasitwam gives him the power over all wild animals; and by mastering *Ishatwam* he can resuscitate the dead.

To the westerner this will sound fantastic and be dismissed as nonsense but I have seen a yogi submerge in a lake for well over five minutes and emerge without the least sign of breathlessness; and I've seen them draw a circle on the ground, round a man and defy him to step out of it. On each occasion he was powerless to do so.

If ever we master such powers and perform such miracles we will realize the futility of power, as they do, and will desire naught but contentment and peace of mind and fusion with the source of ultimate power, which we call Nirvana.

INDEX

145